THE
BOOK
DIRECT
PLAYBOOK

MARK SIMPSON

 Instagram.com/boostlyuk

 Facebook.com/boostlyuk

 Linkedin/in/marksimpson

 Twitter.com/boostlyuk

CONTENTS

CHAMPION MINDSET...................................... **5**

The Warm Up 7

About This Book 11

Get To Know Your Coach 17

Ready For Kick-Off? 19

Get Your Kit Together.. 21

FIRST HALF **25**

Customer Avatar 29

Identifying Your Ideal Guest 37

How To Find Your Ideal Guest.................................. 45

How To Score With Your Ideal Guests 55

Setting Up Your Property, Properly............................ 63

Your Website Is 'The Keystone' 69

To Blog Or Not To Blog?.. 95

The Domain Name 99

SECOND HALF **109**

It's Not What You Know, It's Who You Know.......................... 113

Working With Local Businesses................................. 119

Referral Schemes And Kickbacks 123

More Corporate Bookings...................................... 131

Social Media Secret Sauce 141

The Simple Guide To Content Creation 145

Hashtags & Visibility... 157

Email Marketing.. 165

How To Grow Your Email List.. 173

How To Make The OTAs Work For You 179

Google Is The Next Big OTA 191

The Guest Booking Process 195

Squad Goals 217

ACKNOWLEDGMENTS....................................... 219

THE
BOOK DIRECT
PLAYBOOK

THE WARM UP

NEVER BUILD YOUR HOUSE ON SOMEONE ELSE'S LAND

I will never forget these words. First said to me in the breezy summer of 2011; I had just returned to the UK and back to the family business.

A fourteen-bedroom guesthouse, amid the green landscapes of Harwood Dale village. **The Grainary**, it was called - our family's pride and joy.

My task was to take the business online and effectively, 'spread the word'.

Back then, I thought it was brilliant that websites such as Booking. com, Expedia and, more recently, Airbnb existed. A place where hospitality accommodation businesses were promised 'help' as well as a decent income, so long as they had a stash of good photos of their shiny rooms; and some keyword-stuffed descriptions to match.

'We are partners' these Online Travel Agencies would say.

The problem was (is) that they are anything *but*.

We, as the business owners, are *just* a number to them.

Just another property among the millions of others who sign up to their website.

Just another means of making money, because they only pay us when we get a booking *for them.*

Just another vehicle of their greater, expansive plan; because remember - even when we do get a booking, we have to pay a percentage of the cost back (to them!).

I could go on, but I'm sure you get my drift.

You see, when my parents first opened their guest house in the 90s, there was no such thing as 'commission'. You simply paid to have your business listed in newspapers and magazines, and that was that.

But when the commission model *did* emerge, it disrupted the entire industry. So much so that over the last decade, every listing site has adopted it (and made a good buck along the way).

I see it a lot within the communities I'm a part of. The idea of, '*I don't have to pay anything if it doesn't work*' lulls you into a false sense of security. What's worse, is that it's so easy to get sucked in when listing sites with billions of advertising spend are shouting from every digital rooftop, and encouraging you to join.

The end result? You end up relying on them *heavily* for your bookings.

Which brings me back to that life-changing quote.

A friend of mine, who has been in business for many years, had sent it to me as a reminder - at the perfect time.

'*Never build your house on somebody else's land.*'

To me it means, never rely on one platform for all your income.

Especially if it's a platform you have no ownership over; and frankly, cannot control. It's worse than putting all your eggs in one basket, because you don't even get to be the person who carries that basket around.

However, the biggest problem is, five years since (and after coaching thousands of hosts from all over the world), I've learnt that *this* is exactly what's happening in our industry.

In fact, very recently, while writing this book, I spoke to a host who relied on Airbnb for 95% of their bookings.

That same host is now no longer in business.

So, now is the time to take action, and this playbook is a great place to start.

In it I've poured all my experience, learnings, insights (and the odd soccer reference), to help you finally regain control and turn your business into *the champion* of direct bookings.

You're gonna love it.

Game on.

THE
BOOK DIRECT
PLAYBOOK

ABOUT THIS BOOK

The next few chapters are your open field

The offside rule is allegedly the most 'controversial' in soccer. Of course, this becomes even more complicated when you start talking about the American version (football); and words like 'scrimmage' come into the mix.

As much as I love soccer, I decided early on that there would be no such rules in this playbook. Apart from the fact that it would have to be **100% honest.** No compromises there.

Seriously, don't even feel compelled to read this book in order (from beginning to end). The purpose of the next few chapters is to serve you, so that you can generate more direct bookings. What it shouldn't feel like is a damning chore to get through - because that's no way to learn (nor live for that matter).

So, if there's a specific issue regarding hospitality marketing that's bothering you, then feel free to skip right ahead.

Looking for tips on how to make the most of Google? I have you covered on page 191.

My point is, this playbook is yours to dip-and-dive into, *as well as* read like a novel while you're curled up next to the fire - if that's what you prefer.

I should add, it's imperative that you get through all the content at some point - even if you believe that you already know it. This is because I'll be sharing tips from different personal and professional experiences. All of these experiences are unique to (only) me; and will be of immense value to you and your short-term rental business.

Pull up those socks, as you'll learn:

- How to find and attract your ideal guest and customer

- How to avoid the key killer-mistakes that many hosts make when designing their direct bookings website

- How to become the go-to guy or gal, in your local network

- How to minimise the chances of your guests booking with an online travel agent, ever again!

- How to turn your guests into superfans who will publicly praise your business and become your number one referral system

- Ultimately, how to DOUBLE your direct bookings with simple advice that you can act on, today!

To help you become even bigger Short Term Rental champs, this playbook will be accompanied by an online course that I've personally created for you. It's packed with tutorial videos, templates, and stellar tools for you to use in your business. Best of all, it's FREE.

All you need to do is upload a copy of your receipt via

bookdirectplaybook.com

I magine how different this book would have read, if I'd written it before the year 2020.

Indeed, the universe works in extraordinary ways; because it's only since the dawn of 2020 (and the outbreak of you-know-what) we have realised the true importance of building a direct bookings business.

Which in-turn makes this playbook a Godsend for thousands of STR business owners.

It also means, that I sat down to write it at *the most* befitting moment. (See what the universe did there?)

But let's skip right back to March, 2020. The coronavirus had reached its peak and the entire world was in calamity. In an instant, an industry which for decades has put food on the tables of people like me and you, crumbled down to its very core. And at this moment, I couldn't help but be reminded of the film *Infinity War*, from the Marvel Avengers franchise.

The Marvel Avengers films are by far my favourite, of many. To those of you who haven't watched *Infinity War*, be warned - I am going to butcher the story for you. In time you'll realise that it's all for a good cause.

So, one of the most gripping moments in *Infinity War* is when Thanos (the bad guy) wipes out half of the entire universe's population by simply clicking his fingers. It's pretty intense stuff.

Now imagine, in March 2020, planet Earth's 'Thanos' was Airbnb.

With a simple click of their figurative fingers, this heavyweight OTA wiped out thousands of pounds worth of revenue, for hosts all over the world. These hosts were being faced with the news of COVID-19 spreading, and countries being forced to introduce strict travel bans. Many of these hosts were mothers, fathers, brothers, and sisters - who were *simultaneously* dealing with the reality of their loved ones contracting a serious infection.

Amid all this devastation, Airbnb sent out a generic push-notification to their entire database. Can you believe this was as opposed to reaching out to their hosts empathetically? The irony is, they refer to these hosts as their 'partners'.

Short-term rental professionals worldwide will never forget March, 2020. This was the day mobile phones thundered with bad news thanks to Airbnb. Guests were categorically informed that:

> They could cancel their bookings at no cost, nor penalties. Regardless of any stated cancellation policies, booked guests could cancel - completely free of charge.

Even writing that today makes me feel like I have a heavy ball rolling across my chest.

Imagine the catastrophe. But then again, many of you have had to live through this horror, firsthand.

Facebook groups, Twitter threads, Reddit forums, were all packed to-the-seams with panicked messages.

> 'I can't speak to my guests'

> 'It's impossible for me to change bookings and salvage any kind of revenue'

> 'I have woken up to empty calendars and zero revenue'

There were cancellations upon cancellations, and not a single solution. In a poorly-planned attempt to communicate with travellers, Airbnb completely disregarded property hosts and owners - the very people that have carried this OTA to enormous success.

During this time of the pandemic, cancellations were, of course, unavoidable. However, the key difference between direct bookings and bookings via Airbnb was (and is) **control.** Yet another 'c-word' that determined the fate of thousands of industry professionals.

The thing is, hosts who had direct bookings were easily able to reach out independently to their guests.

Able to have a conversation with them.

Able to change, rather than cancel their stay.

Able to save their businesses.

In fact, I'll give you a black-and-white example. At The Grainary (our family business, if you remember) we saved tens of thousands of pounds in revenue, on that dreary day in March. This was simply because our bookings were made directly through the business - and not via Airbnb, nor any other OTA.

We moved a large majority of our guests' bookings to 2021; and, more importantly, we *personally* assured our guests that we would do everything humanly possible to keep them safe and to keep them in-the-loop. Never underestimate the value of old-fashioned communication in our industry.

But sadly, many other businesses were not as lucky. They paid the heavy price of playing by somebody else's rules. It was like playing a soccer match and having a referee who blatantly favours the opposing team. These poor STR operators had already set themselves up to lose.

However, they are not to blame. It's clear-as-day that short-term rental businesses are better off with more direct bookings; but the process of HOW to get them, remains an enigma.

Until now.

That day in March was a lightbulb moment for me. But in retrospect, this book has been ten hardcore years in the making. It is the result of nearly a lifetime spent in hospitality, knee-deep in all its nooks and crannies; through the good times and the bad.

You're reading this sentence because you realise the need for more direct bookings.

I am here to show you, it *can* be done.

You *can* earn bigger profits. You *can* get more power.

You *can* grab the reins of your STR business and control the entire guest journey, with pride.

You *can*, you *can*, you *can*.

Take this as the pre-match pep talk that you've always wanted. Remember, nobody else is going to take responsibility for your short-term rental business for you.

But for now, you have everything you need. **Right here.**

GET TO KNOW YOUR COACH

AKA 'Mark Simpson' (AKA, Me!)

In case you haven't figured it out already, I'm a soccer fanatic. This glorious sport has remained my first love and passion - as well as Liverpool Football Club, of course! In fact, you'll often find me at the first and last home game of every season; a tradition I've kept up since my Grandad took me to my very first match, back in '98.

Speaking of family - I'm BIG on this stuff. I'm Dad to three brilliant boys, Alfie, Charlie, and Frankie and husband to Laura Nicholson Simpson, who's patiently dealt with my many 'phases' while I've been writing this book. Thanks, Laura.

As a family, we've travelled plenty - the world three times over, to be precise!

On the business side of things, I founded Boostly (my company) in 2016 off-the-back of the lack of support provided to hospitality businesses, on a local and accessible level. I'm a doer, if there's a problem that I know I can solve, then you won't catch me wasting time complaining about it.

To date, the Boostly Website Company remains one of the largest agencies (of its kind) in the world - and our Training Academy is one of the *only* officially accredited ones for the short-term rental industry. This is all with enormous thanks to my team; and all the talented people who work so hard behind-the-scenes.

Throughout my career, I've had the honour of professionally speaking at some of the biggest hospitality events across the globe. I'm also the host of an award-winning podcast (Boostly Podcast), that is frequently ranked among the Top 50 UK podcasts. I guess my killer-knack for speaking endlessly has been of great use there!

If you fancy stalking me (and my work) before diving into this book, then check out the following handles:

Instagram.com/boostlyuk

Facebook.com/boostlyuk

Linkedin/in/marksimpson

Twitter.com/boostlyuk

READY FOR KICK-OFF?

Final points to help you bring your A-Game

I rarely read books from beginning to end. For me, information is a lot easier to absorb when it's in bite-sized pieces and laid out in a way where I can simply dip and dive in my spare time - as I please.

I'm sure many of you will be on a similar wavelength.

That's why I've designed this book so that it appeals to you as well.

Hopefully, even the most unconventional type of time-poor readers will gain instant value from the Book Direct Playbook, so that they can go ahead and action all the good stuff in their STR businesses. So, don't worry if you don't have those extra two hours to spare every day (nor even the patience) for a big old clunky book. Because that is not what this is.

I've actually taken inspiration from two of my favourite books of all time (highly recommended, by the way). *Tools of Titans* by Tim Ferris and *The Rules of Life* by Richard Templer - both of which I've hungrily devoured over one hundred times.

I have copies of these two reads in both my car and home and every time I have five minutes to spare, I open the book(s) at random, and read a small section. This, without fail, gives me the mojo I need - then I can go ahead and implement the advice that I've just learned from. Remember, there's no point learning new things, if you don't implement them later.

I'd love for you to do the same with this book.

Of course, you're more than welcome to read it like a story (in order); but even if you could take just a few minutes to dip your head into it every day (and more importantly, **action** my advice), then that'd make the last year of relentlessly writing this book worthwhile.

Think of it like a sports playbook. The coach doesn't go through every page before finding a play to run for his team.

Instead, he finds a specific play - one that'll immediately improve the overall game - and puts it into action straight away.

So, in the same way, you might want to take a moment to have a think about what you feel you need most help with first, for your short-term rental business. Then, navigate to the right section of this playbook, and get your A-Game on instantly. Whether it's support with systems, email marketing, or social media, this book covers the must-know tips for everything.

GET YOUR KIT TOGETHER

This playbook covers everything your business needs to become a direct bookings machine.

But, is your head in the game? Here's a quick run-through of things that you might need to remember, to get maximum benefit from the next few chapters:

- **Something to make notes on:** Action is what matters. It's likely that this book will spark loads of ideas for your STR business. Write (or type) everything down - this will form a plan that you can actually implement later.

- **Speak like a pro:** We'll be using a lot of industry-specific lingo in this Playbook. It'll be useful to get your head around the basics.

- **Grab the Audible version of this playbook:** This is a GENIUS productivity hack. I recently learned that listening to the audio version of books, while *simultaneously* reading them, helps consume information in a much faster, and much more efficient way. If you're serious about getting your game on, I strongly recommend **going through** both versions of the Book Direct Playbook.

- **Sign up for the FREE Book Direct Playbook Course:** I've personally designed a free course to accompany the Book Direct Playbook. Follow this along to really leverage what you learn in this book. We'll be dishing up free video tutorials, templates, tools, the lot! All you need to do is head to bookdirectplaybook.com.

- **Join the Hospitality Community Facebook Group:** You'll have immediate access to this private group (simply search, and request to join), where you'll have the chance to connect with other hosts and share ideas.

- **Know your short-term rental business:** Squad, I'm here to support you every step of the way. But it's vital that you understand your own business as well (it's incredible - many don't). The tips in this book are based on years of hospitality experience and working with thousands of STR professionals all over the world. Much of the advice is universal (can be applied to any STR business); however, there will be times when you'll need to slightly 'tweak' certain processes, to suit your demographic and location.

I'm not the kind of guy who'll write a book for you, and disappear into a black hole of corporate nothingness after.

Keep me in-the-loop while you're working through this playbook by messaging me on Instagram @boostlyuk or sharing your playbook experiences on social media, with the hashtag #teamboostly

We've got this, team!

GET YOUR KIT TOGETHER

SPEAK LIKE A PRO

OTA	Online Travel Agency (the likes of Airbnb, Booking.com, etc)
STR	Short Term Rental (the UK term for 'vacation rentals')
PMS	Property Management Software
GID	Get It Done
SEO	Search Engine Optimization
CTA	Call To Action
DM	Direct Message / Private Message
FPG	Future Potential Guest

FIRST
HALF

THE
BOOK DIRECT
PLAYBOOK

Let me know that you're reading this book.

Send me a message on

Instagram.com/boostlyuk

THE
BOOK DIRECT
PLAYBOOK

CUSTOMER AVATAR

What you'll read below is a scripted account of a conversation I had with Dan Meredith, back in 2016.

Actually, it's paraphrased (i.e. minus the swear words), because I know my Mum will read this book. And just to assure you, yes *it is* relevant to customer avatars.

Just stay with me.

To give you some background info, Dan has been - and remains - one of the biggest influences in my business.

Although he has a tendency to rip you a new one (especially after saying the words *'I say this with a smile on my face'*), this guy has an unbelievable knack of identifying the very root of your business problem - quicker than you can look it up on Google.

The conversation below is what went on between Dan and I during one of his infamous 'Hot Seat Calls'.

Back then, a group of 40-60 business owners - all at different stages of their business journey - would gather on a webinar call hosted by Dan, and take it in turns to be verbally torn apart by him. All for our own respective benefit, of course.

I would love listening to my peers getting grilled but when it came round to my turn - oh boy, my hands would literally shake with nerves!

Thank goodness those calls were only on audio, so nobody could see how red in the face I'd go!

Me: Dan, I'm stuck. I don't know how to best describe what I do.

Dan: Well, what are you doing? How would you explain it to me if I had just met you at a bar?

Me: I help business owners with their marketing.

Dan: No.

Me: ...

(awkward silence)

Dan: That means nothing to me, and it'll mean nothing to your ideal clients. Try again.

Me: ...

(another awkward silence, now getting embarrassing)

Dan: Look, who do you directly help?

Me: Short stay accommodation owners, in hospitality.

Dan: Good. Try again.

Me: I help short stay accommodation owners with their marketing.

Dan: NO.

I should point out, I was literally *sweating* at this point. All the blood rushing through me was making my face turn from an acceptable shade of red to an astonishing bright purple. I just kept thinking to myself *'I would rather be ANYWHERE right now, rather than at this virtual grilling.'*

I'd be lying if I said I wasn't tempted to press the *'Leave Meeting'* button; and I probably might've done, if I didn't have to face the embarrassment of then showing up in the Facebook group - among the very people who'd just witnessed my car crash of a call.

But ultimately, I didn't want to let Dan down.

I didn't want to let *myself* down.

After all, I had joined the **'Coffee with Dan'** Facebook Group because I was serious about creating a business that offered support to hospitality owners - as it was so *shockingly lacking* in my local area of Scarborough, UK.

This wonderfully bearded man, who was more than capable of making grown adults cry, was simply trying to help me. And might I add, he knew *exactly* what he was doing during our Hot Seat call.

You see, Dan smells self-defecating BS way before the average human. He almost has a talent for it. It's an amazing quality to have in a business owner, as well as a published author (which he is too, by the way).

Dan wasn't giving me a grilling because he got some kind of an egoistic kick out of it. But because it was important that I said these words for myself - Dan knew I had it in me all along; and that's what makes him an epic coach.

> **Me:** I give short stay accommodation owners the tools, tactics, training and confidence to get direct bookings for their business, and not overly rely on OTAs.

Till this day, I have no idea where that came from.

It was one of those 'eureka moments' that clever people talk about on TV.

That one penalty shoot-out that changes the entire trajectory of a soccer game.

I sure as hell wrote those words down, as soon as they left my mouth - and have used them to define my niche ever since.

I became 'The Book Direct Guy' - which is why you're now reading 'The Book Direct Playbook'.

And do you know something, squad? Things began to fall into place after that.

Every email I sent, every podcast I wrote, every word I read (or spoke) was delivered with **more direct bookings** concretely in mind. Essentially, it became the engine that was driving all my ideas and marketing. The problem I was solving was as clear as day: to no longer rely on platforms such as Airbnb, Booking.com, and Expedia to generate bookings.

I'd found my niche! Eureka, I'd found my niche!

Linking this back to the actual title of this chapter, **'Customer Avatar'** - I'd like you to begin to understand how important it is to identify your target audience, just as I did during my call with Dan.

Granted, my example was for Boostly and not a short stay accommodation business; but the principle remains the same:

WHEN YOU TRY TO APPEAL TO EVERYONE, YOU APPEAL TO NO-ONE

'The riches are the niches' as we so commonly read on social media memes. Hey, it's a cliché but it speaks 100% sense. You cannot possibly expect to reach phenomenal business results if you try to please everyone - all you'll end up being is safe, boring, and vanilla. (And nobody's going to remember that).

You see, once I'd carved out my niche, I doubled-down on it and then my tribe came to me. That's the beauty of knowing who it actually is you're speaking to. Within six months, membership of **The Hospitality Community** (my free Facebook Group) DOUBLED - and word continued to spread like wildfire.

Eventually, the global members of my group became eloquently versed when it came to describing what I do - and that's exactly what you need to achieve for your hospitality business.

GET IT DONE

Hey, hello! We're taking a break from absorbing information (as fun as that is), so I can ask you to do something for me.

For the record, I'll be scattering these Get it Done sessions throughout the Playbook, to help you to action the advice that I'm giving you.

Okay, here we go. First of all, I need you to ensure that you've read the content prior to this Get it Done section *in this chapter* so far. Otherwise, you'll fail to fully appreciate the point of the task that I'm going to set for you.

So, Dan helped me all those years ago...let's see if I can try and pay it forward.

I want you to get your phone ready to send me a DM on Instagram.

Next, I want you to search for @boostlyuk on Instagram. A simple search will do, you should find the profile straight away.

Then, I want you to send me a quick message telling me who your ideal guest is.

Do it right now (as long as it's safe for you to do so).

After that, all I want you to do is go through the rest of this chapter and see if your answer changes. Sounds easy enough, right?

Of course, you might be thinking at this point *'But Mark, I don't know who my ideal guest is.'*

Or worse:

**'My ideal guest is one who pays me money!'
(Dear lord, no).**

But send me a message anyway. I promise I won't be as brazen as Dan was with me - and this truly will help you identify your ideal guest.

Not Every Guest's The Goal

One of the biggest disadvantages of working with online travel agents is that you have zero control over what guests they send you. Just imagine, they could send you world-class raveaholics; and there's nothing you'd be able to do about it.

As a result, a big chunk of guests (courtesy of OTAs) could fail to 'fit your property' - which as it happens, is a section we're going to cover later on in this chapter.

But let's dig down on this 'ideal guest' concept some more.

Picture the perfect guest arriving at your property; whatever they may look like to you.

They frolic into your beautiful building, and you immediately receive a text message from them praising your decor and attention to detail. Heaven.

Upon checking out, your guests leave your property in immaculate condition and leave a review that is frankly, one of the best you've ever received.

It's like your short-stay accommodation and their personality is a match made in heaven; and it feels as though you've welcomed a friend into your home, rather than a guest into your business.

While it may sound too good to be true, this is exactly what happens when you nail-down your customer avatar. This wonderful hospitality dream could easily become a regular occurrence for you.

It's a simple principle:

There are 7.7 billion people on this planet.

You only have a minimal amount of space to fill.

You don't need to appeal to all 7.7 billion people.

You only need to appeal to a minuscule fraction of them.

This break-down of your customer avatar is by far the most important part of this entire Playbook. So, take heed of the next few sections because not only am I going to help you identify your ideal guests, I'm going to show you exactly how you can find them, too.

By the end of it, you'll be screaming 'SCOOORE!' every time a direct booking lands into your business inbox.

THE
BOOK DIRECT
PLAYBOOK

IDENTIFYING YOUR IDEAL GUEST

'I don't know where to start' was the response from a Boostly Academy student.

She was stuck.

We had just completed the **Discovering Your Ideal Guest** training and 600 other members were getting things done. Happily, ticking things off their checklist.

Then, the above phrase popped up - in the form of a public post. And straight away, dozens of supportive Boostly members scurried into the comments section to offer positive pep-talks, as well as advice and ideas. This was one of the many times I'd felt immensely proud of the community we'd created.

Now, the struggle for this student is, of course, a common one.

The dreaded question of WHERE. TO. BEGIN?

Or even more frightening, *'Do I know who my ideal guest is?'*

Believe it or not, I hear the answer of *'a paying one'* more times than I'd like to admit. But over the years, I've realised that it starts off by asking yourself the following things:

- Where is your property located?

- What is the 80/20 split of people who visit this area?

- What is your property set up for?

- What amenities do you offer?

- What's in your local vicinity?

As it happens, this topic always takes me back to a movie I love and have watched countless times. *Field of Dreams* starring Kevin Costner.

In the movie, Costner builds a baseball field in the middle of his cornfield, attracting the ghosts of baseball legends (epic). One of the standout lines from the blockbuster is **'If you build it, they will come'** and in true Hollywood style - against all odds, of course - spectators do show up to watch.

Clearly, life isn't one big movie. And I understand that it isn't as easy as building a business and waiting for the money to come rolling in. Otherwise everybody would be doing it, right?

In real life, we need to be strategic. However, if we build things strategically (with our end-consumers in mind), then there's a pretty good chance that we'll begin to attract more and more people.

In fact, I guarantee that you can now think of a certain date or event - coming up later in the year - and know that you could sell-out five times over, if you really wanted to. The problem is, there'd likely be many guests who'd book into your property - but not actually be the right 'fit' for you.

So, I'm going to show you how to nip this problem in the bud. Think of yourself as Neo from *The Matrix* movie. You know, the main hero who has the ability to freely manipulate the (simulated) reality of the matrix? Basically, the guy with a lot of strategic power who will start seeing the 1 and 0 fill your screen, while no Agent Smith will be able to lay a finger on you, while you navigate through this world of sleek marketing.

Bare with me as I get excited by all the movie references and help you take that 'red pill'. Essentially, I'm your Morpheus in this section of the Playbook, and I'm going to guide you out of this rabbit hole.

GET IT DONE

Right, are you ready for another Get it Done sesh?

This time, I want you to grab a sheet of paper or notebook. Anything you can scribble on.

Then, jot down all the events that are taking place in your local area over the next twelve months. At the same time, write down what your area - in particular - is known for. This could be anything (food, culture, landmarks).

Now, there's a fantastic resource for this Get it Done session, buried away in **Facebook Ads Manager**. Don't worry, it's completely free to access; and it'll give you ALL the information you need.

If you need additional help with finding this, I've recorded a video in the accompanying Book Direct Playbook course which you can check out now by visiting: bookdirectplaybook.com (registering won't cost you a penny).

Once you're on the platform, head on over to Chapter Two. There, you'll find a video that'll show you how to use Facebook Ads Manager to pinpoint an audience to anyone on Facebook who has visited your area in the past year. It's clever stuff!

Ads Manager will also show you the most popular Facebook Pages that this audience 'Likes'. So, you'll be able to note down their average age, their gender, and their general interests.

After you've done the above, you'll need to go and find out who are the **20%** of your guests who bring in **80%** of your fantastic reviews.

The Pareto Principle

In a nutshell: 80% of consequences comes from 20% of causes (the 'vital few'). This principle is also known as the 80/20 Rule, or The Principle of Factor Sparsity. But that last one's a bit of a mouthful.

Anyway, in a hospitality context, The Pareto Principle could focus on: **Which 20% of your guests bring in 80% of your best reviews.** Do you see what we're doing here? Thinking like business owners and strategically analysing our guests.

So, to work out your 80/20 figures, you'll need to visit the review website that brings in the most reviews. Then, you'll need to filter your reviews until you can see the five-star ones.

Then, you'll need to read each one (we're slipping back into **Get it Done** territory here).

What you're looking for in these reviews are **recurring keywords**.

Let me give you an example:

1 | The bed was amazing. So comfy.

2 | The local pubs were all top-class. Would definitely come again!

3 | The safety of the property offered real peace-of-mind. My children could run free, and we didn't have to worry.

While each positive review speaks of a different demographic, you'll notice that the running theme is safety and family-friendliness. From this, we can comfortably assume that you're mainly attracting families to your short-stay accommodation.

So, if your goal was to appeal to more adults and young couples, then you would need to tweak your marketing accordingly - and you could continue to monitor if it's working, by using the same method.

Let's have another example:

Your customer avatar is contractors. How are you going to ensure that your marketing speaks to this demographic? The words you use here will, as ever, be extremely important.

It'd be pointless to use something like:

'Your ideal weekend getaway' as your homepage headline, or across your social media pages.

Because contractors normally stay at short-stay accommodation mid-week.

Instead, it'd make more sense to have something like:

'The Comforts of Home, While You Work'

See how in an instant you're directly speaking to your target demographic here? You don't need to be an English major to figure this out.

Contractors want home comforts and convenience at the end of a hard day's work. Amenities like safe and secure parking, so that they can unpack their van after a long day (and have a place to store their things, without making a mess in your property).

They want a big fridge to store food.

They want at least one bath for every two beds, per property.

They want good and reliable WiFi, Netflix, and perhaps some sports channels on TV.

And if you can sort them out with takeaway menus and a couple of crates of beer as well - then all the better.

The headline above insinuates all this; so you'll be far more likely to appeal to your customer avatar.

GET IT DONE

This session will require some teamwork, squad.

This is what you do: visit your website homepage and look at the **'above the fold'** section. Above the fold is clever marketing speak for the bit on your homepage that visitors instantly see, without scrolling down the page.

Now, grab your laptop and show this section of your homepage to someone who doesn't know your business that well, ideally someone who's never seen your website before - **or better,** a child between the age of eight to ten. (Kids are so unfiltered, their honesty is a big help in business).

Open your laptop, and then close it after four seconds.

Then ask your lovely team mates:

'Based on what the website says, what do I do and who am I speaking to?'

I'm going to reiterate: asking a child would be a big help here, because as a rule of thumb, basic marketing copy should be (mostly) understood by a 9 year-old anyway. If it totally escapes them, then that's a red flag for you to revisit and simplify.

Of course, if you're struggling to find someone to help you for this session visit usertesting.com where you can pay a small amount for this service.

Ultimately, all we want is an honest answer.

Ideally, that answer should match who you want your ideal guests to be.

If this isn't the case, then that's no problem either. It means that we've noticed the issue in good time; and we're ready to make some productive changes.

For further help, I've uploaded yet another video on bookdirectplaybook.com which will help you crack this (perfectly). I strongly recommend that you head on over to the website to complete this task, before working through any other section of this chapter.

Go get 'em!

HOW TO FIND YOUR IDEAL GUEST

Alright, this is the fun part. To get the most out of this chapter, you'll definitely need to have worked out who your ideal guests are. Remember, it's perfectly okay to have more than one customer avatar so long as you know them as well as your best friends. Likes, dislikes, fears, goals - that sort of thing.

The prior sections of this chapter have amplified the importance of **finding a niche** and understanding that by appealing to everyone, you ultimately appeal to no-one. Be sure to put this learning to good use now. It's gonna pay you back, ten-fold.

I'll be using another example to help get my point across here. It's actually more of a **story** than a rigid example. Because as I've recently started preaching to my Academy members and every person in the STR community:

THERE'S A STORY BEHIND EVERY BOOKING

(A quote you'll be hearing a lot of throughout this Playbook. It makes you think, what are the events that lead up to that sweet, direct booking? What's the story?)

So, here's a family profile to help us set the scene:

Let's go with a UK based family, who love staycations.
They like to travel to the beach but also love to explore the countryside.

For the purpose of this story, let's call the parents Sarah and Mike. Now, both Sarah and Mike are self-employed and can work from virtually anywhere, so long as they have a Wifi connection and their laptops.

Combined, they have an annual income of 50k+ and they currently live in the city. When it comes to travelling, the main priority is fun for their three children (but also, to have ample space to explore).

Sarah is the decision-maker in the family; although Mike likes to believe he is. Bless him.

Now that we're up-to-speed with the family, we can begin.

The question is: how am I going to get my property in front of Sarah and Mike?

MAKE SURE YOUR PROPERTY IS EVERYWHERE

This is the single, most important rule.

Blanket approach.

Make sure you have as many touch points as possible. Literally, covering all bases.

I'm going to walk you through this step-by-step so that you can get your head around it, fully. There's also a video showing you exactly what we're going to cover over on the accompanying online course: bookdirectplaybook.com. Be sure to check this out as well.

So, the premise is simple.

Google is your friend here.

For this part of the Playbook, you'll need to power up Google on your computer and select **Private Mode**. A simple Google search will show you how to do this, if you don't already know (YouTube will have some handy videos, too).

As you'll already know, there are tons of website browsers, and they all have a different name for their version of 'Private Mode'. From Google's perspective, essentially all you need to understand is that Google collects your information every time you use its browser. But Private Mode doesn't track anything; it treats you as though you're using Google for the first time.

Anyway, once you have loaded up Private Mode, you'll need to perform 10 different searches.

In total, we'll do 3 variations of these searches; so you'll end up with 30 different results.

As there's a lot of data involved in this task, it'd be wise for you to open up a spreadsheet on your computer as well - or use a pen and paper, if you wish. Just something to jot your findings down on.

All ready?

Right, the first 10 searches you're going to carry out will be for generic searches around your area.

For example:

- Accommodation in Scarborough

- B&B in Scarborough

- Hotel in Scarborough

- Places to stay in Scarborough

… and so on.

For inspiration on the kind of searches people are typing into Google right now, check the video on bookdirectplaybook.com (where you can get help with this, for free). I've recorded a video especially for this bit, and it'll help you loads.

So, once you've started carrying out your searches you'll need to make a note of all the websites that appear **on the first page of Google only.** You might have heard of the saying that you could hide a dead body on page 2 of Google search results? Well, that ought to tell you what a waste of time looking at page 2 is.

What you're going to do is make a note of all the websites that appear on page 1 and put a gate next to it.

Then, you're going to run the next search on your list.

And rinse and repeat. And rinse and repeat.

While doing this, you'll want to record which results are **paid**, and which results are **organic**. You'll be able to differentiate between the two easily, because the paid search results will have the text 'ad' next to them. (But do check out the accompanying training course for this Playbook if you still feel overwhelmed).

By the time you've gotten round to search number 10, you'll have noticed a recurring theme. But before casting any assumptions, it's best to run the next batch of 10 searches.

This time, we could focus on the county/state - or wider area.

So, for example:

- Hotel in Yorkshire

- Accommodation in Yorkshire

- Rental accommodation in Yorkshire

- Places to stay in Yorkshire

- Airbnbs in Yorkshire

Once again, you'll be using the wonders of Google to get a digital snapshot of what people are searching for, right now. While also making a note of what you find - and celebrating what a joy the internet is.

For the final 10 rounds of searches, I want you to focus on your **niche.**

So, let's return to our UK based family to serve as an example... Mike and Sarah (and the kids).

For them, I would be searching things like:

- Family friendly accommodation in Yorkshire

- Family friendly accommodation in Scarborough

- Places to stay for families in Scarborough

- Accommodation with good wifi Yorkshire

- Digital nomad recommendations in Yorkshire

Now, anybody who knows me, knows that I'm a stickler for data. There's great benefit to this, because the more data you have access to, the better your understanding of your demographic and industry. However, I do have a tendency to get carried away at the best of times and run searches within the digits of 20, 30, or even 40.

If you're not as obsessed with data as me, rest assured you can get away with running a minimum of 10 searches.

Either way, your focus here should be the 80/20 rule - or the **Pareto Principle**, as explained earlier on in this chapter.

Which 20% of websites are appearing, 80% of the time?

Now, for every location, the result is going to be different. It's paramount that you understand this.

I have to admit, one of the most annoying pet peeves I have online (within Facebook Groups and suchlike) is when somebody comes in and asks:

'Which website(s) should I be listing on? I have heard of platform X, so I guess I should be listing on there?'

Then a bunch of people flock to the person's question and recommend a whole host of sites - which by the way, are completely irrelevant.

Everything is location and niche specific. It's as subjective as what a good goalkeeper means to you. It depends on a BUNCH of stuff.

So, the smarter way to address the aforementioned question is to revisit your search results (which you'll have made a tidy record of in your spreadsheet or notepad), and identify the core group of 20% websites that have appeared 80% of the time.

> ## AND IF YOU AREN'T LISTED ON THAT 20% THEN GO AND LIST YOUR PROPERTY THERE

It's more than likely that the majority of these options will be commission related. And while I can hear you calling *'But this is a Playbook for direct bookings, Mark!'* - I want you to know that I'm a man with a plan, and we'll 100% cover how to convert these bookings to **direct bookings**, later on in the chapter.

The goal remains the same. But for now, we need to focus on being present everywhere so that we can make ourselves stronger; build all our momentum up, for the action that's yet to come!

So, on the subject of being **E.V.E.R.Y.W.H.E.R.E:**

One of the first things I'd be checking with your channel manager is if they link to said website. A simple call, email, or live chat message will tell you this - no drama. Nice and easy.

Don't panic if this is not the case with your channel manager, it's definitely not the end of the world and all can be resolved. Normally, under these circumstances, your channel manager will use this as an opportunity to reach out to the website in question, and establish a partnership on your behalf.

Win. Win. Win.

On some occasions, you'll come across a website where you'll need to pay to be listed. This is, of course, a separate conversation; but for what it's worth my opinion is that the return on investment could be huge for you. Sometimes you have to spend money to make loads more of it. But I'll show you how to do this in a way that maximises your chances of boosting your ROI.

For these paid websites, there's a high chance that they *won't* directly link to your channel manager. However, this isn't much of an issue because they'll be using a phone call or email as a trackable referral from the listing site.

Once you have cracked Google friends, you'll need to move onto social media channels.

Use the same approach we've practiced at the top of this section to search on Facebook (for Facebook Groups) within your local area and niche. Then, join 3-5 groups that fit into this category.

I'll cover the nitty-gritties of leveraging social media and social media groups in the **Second Half** of this Playbook. But for now, you need to remember to keep a keen eye on the groups you've just joined. Add them to your 'favourites' in your bookmarks, as well as on your phone notes.

Look to spend 10-15 minutes a day in these groups, quickly scouring for which questions are being asked, what people are looking for, and what enquiries are flooding in. You have a hub of research and valuable information at your fingertips - learn from it, and store it in your business memory bank for later.

After you've covered Google search and social media, we'll have two more things to do. Now's a good time to grab a sip of water if you need it...

The next step is to open up a Google search, and this time look for podcasts around your niche.

My bet is that you weren't expecting this tip, right?

But there are over **1 million active podcasts in the world**, and *every* generation *of every* demographic known to man is listening to them. Podcasts are the only form of content that is not disruptive, hence their increasing popularity. If you're watching a video or reading a blog at some point, you may need to stop to do something else.

But with a podcast, you can multitask. Absorb all those juicy insights while walking the dog, driving into town, or making the bed. This is exactly why I started the Boostly Podcast in 2016, and it's now one of the biggest UK podcasts for business and marketing.

To summarise, podcasts are epic. Don't be so quick to dismiss them.

Once you've found podcasts around your niche and reach (which I'm sure you will, after some digging), find out if they're welcoming guests. This could be a remarkable opportunity for you. Who knows, a podcast interview could get listened to by thousands of Mikes and Sarahs, making you get inundated with bookings! This stuff is certainly not unheard of.

For the final part of this section, I want you to take things offline. See if you can find any print magazines, newspapers, books etc, that your ideal guests would read.

Let me tell you, whatever these digital day-and-age folk preach to you, **print is not dead.**

Yes, we live in a digitally-driven world, but there is still AMPLE room for print. In fact, depending on your ideal guest, it might even be the most impactful form of advertising for you.

Again, this links back to your survey, and it could even require you picking up the phone and calling your guests if they're part of the Baby Boomer generation and they 'don't do email' as I get to hear soooo many times.

If you're not confident on the phone, write them a letter. (But you should probably work on getting confident on the phone at some point).

You see, the best thing about appearing in print magazines, books, and newspapers is that currently, the cost of it is very low. And if you time it at the right point in the sales month, you could bag yourself even more of a bargain as panicked sales reps will be trying to meet targets. Trust me, I speak as an ex Sales Rep and Manager for what was a big publication in my time; the end of a sales quarter was when my office mates would slip into an anxious frenzy and offer insane deals to get them 'over the line' and keep their jobs. It's a tough business.

A bit later on in this Playbook (in the Social Media chapter), I'll show you a cool hashtag tactic where you can discover even more ideal guests.

But before that, let's practice our game with another Get it Done session.

GET IT DONE

Your Get it Done session for this section of the Playbook is to figure out where your ideal guests are 'hanging out' (i.e. spending their valuable time).

What I want you to do is send a Direct Message to me on Instagram **@boostlyuk** with your findings - I'll be waiting in keen anticipation!

You'd actually be amazed by some of the results I've personally discovered since I started coaching back in 2016. Let's see if you can come up with anything more obscure (and hey, the world is a colourful place, so you may well do).

Anyway, now that we've figured out WHO your ideal guests are and where they hang out, let's move onto actually turning those Lookers into Bookers.

HOW TO SCORE WITH YOUR IDEAL GUESTS

It's all well and good knowing who your ideal guests are, and where to find them, but of course, it's needless research if all you're going to do is repel them faster than a soccer ball on fire.

Okay, pretty extreme. But I'm sure you understand my point here.

Turning 'Lookers into Bookers' is where the money-making stuff happens. This is what differentiates a successful hospitality business from an unsuccessful one - so it's imperative that you read the following sections in full (and ACT on them).

So, every month I like to host something called a **Marketing Review Live.**

This is where I randomly pick members of the Hospitality Community Facebook Group and look at their marketing.

I'll always share a post and ask if someone would like for me to look at their marketing and, of course, we always find hundreds of keen hospitality business owners raising their hands. So, I deal with this in the most mature and sensible way I know how and put each of the candidates names into a cereal bowl, and ask one of my kids to pick a name at random. (Family business, you know the drill).

From there, I send the lucky few a Google form to complete, which gives me a little more insight into their business and current circumstances. Following that, I pick a day and go live on social media and we talk through each candidate's situation and respective forms.

The kind of areas we decipher are: book direct websites and social media channels - as well as how they're being viewed by Google.

What drives this entire marketing review is what these candidates tell me about the current circumstances of their hospitality business, and where they would love to be in six months time.

You see, these marketing reviews are epic because they always give me the opportunity to help someone. There's always some way that I can help a fellow hospitality professional, because there's always something to improve and offer constructive feedback on.

The best part is, even the members who are part of the audience of these marketing reviews (and have not been picked from the trusty cereal bowl) have something to learn from too. In fact, I can guarantee that every time I'm breaking down somebody's hospitality business during my live, there are at least 10 other people who can relate to their problems. And that's the beauty of building communities.

On one such occasion, I was speaking to a host.

They were frustrated with the lack of bookings from their website. They could see they were getting the traffic from their Google Analytics report but the number of people who were booking was practically zero.

This poor host couldn't figure out why this was happening.

She was based in a city and, in fact, nicely located to all the local amenities.

She had already worked out that her ideal guests were contractors or business folk.

'A home away from home' she proudly told me.

But the problem was, nobody was booking via her website. Even though there was a lot of traffic going to her website, very few people were actually clicking.

On top of this, this host was paying a heavy commission fee to those pesky OTAs because business guests - as you may already know - like to book for a few weeks at a time. So we needed to help this host, and fast.

We started off by looking at her website.

And man. The answer was right there, staring us right in the face.

I mean, it would've been obvious to anyone who isn't involved in the day-to-day of the business. As business owners we tend to get stuck inside 'a bottle'. Not being able to see from the outside-in; and making clumsy judgements in the process.

On this host's website, there was not one mention of business bookings.

About 'being ideal' for business or corporate guests.

Come to think of it, the entire website was designed for a leisure market with walls upon walls of text talking about the area's nightlife, tourist spots, and things to do over the weekend when the sun's shining outside.

As lovely as that all sounds, this is perhaps the perfect example of how NOT to appeal to your ideal guest.

So, on the aforementioned marketing review, I left this wonderful host some feedback on what I would personally do.

I immediately recommended a content switch-up. Promising to touch base with the host a few weeks later, to see how she'd got on.

A few weeks later this host was indeed beaming with joy.

Bloody beaming.

She'd left me a cheerful WhatsApp voice note to say that she had made the recommended changes to the website copy and she had received her first booking directly from the website: a BIG corporate contract, paying a good price per head, and what's best is that they'd signed up for the whole calendar year.

I took a look at the changes.

And as soon as the page loaded onto my phone, my eyes saw what I'd been longing to see.

The tag line directly spoke to a contractor or business guest.

I was hooked.

Wanted to read more.

I scrolled down the page.

No more talking about days out and walks in the sunshine. The focus now was entirely business.

- Safe and secure parking for big vans.

- Super fast WiFi to get work done and call the family back home.

- Netflix and Amazon Prime TV all got a cheeky mention too.

Plenty of cooking amenities and also a full list of recommended takeaway places within close proximity to the property **PLUS** a QR code with clear instructions on how to use the appliances.

Bus routes and other transport information was also at-hand. It seemed that my job for this part, was done.

The host had gone all in.

She had tapped into what her ideal guest wanted and conveyed exactly that. I'm not exaggerating when I say, it was **perfect**.

Oh, and it didn't just stop there. You see, I scrolled through her social media posts and all the content on there was directly speaking to contractors and business guests, alike.

Simple phrases like:

Long Term Stays

Home Away From Home

The host had also started leveraging LinkedIn because she'd realised that's where the likes of PAs and accommodation liaisons for big companies were more likely to network. She had figured the nooks and crannies of the people she was selling to, to an absolute T.

It was fantastic to see.

All of that would've taken just a few hours to do. All it required was a quick shift in thinking and implementation and it resulted in a mighty big contract - as well as a company wanting more properties like hers.

As a result of this, the host was able to network and find other property hosts in the area and put together a combined package where she would receive kickbacks for every booking that came in from any third-party companies, that she would pass business onto.

The best part, squad?

ZERO COMMISSION COSTS TO THE BIG OTAs

Instead, friendships and partnerships being made via the sweet art of collaboration. Teamwork! As they proudly advocate in soccer.

In all this, the guests were (and will continue to be) exceptionally happy too.

Win.

Win.

Win.

GET IT DONE

Now, it's your turn: **have a browse through your website copy.**

Scroll through your social media posts as well; and be honest with yourself here.

Does the content that you're posting match the needs of your ideal guests?

Or are you just posting content with a scattergun approach, just for the buzz of it?

As mentioned in the earlier section of this Playbook, it's quite possible that you'll have more than one ideal guest demographic, too. So, you might be wondering how to create content that'll appeal to ALL these people?

Your first option is to plaster generic, 'safe' words that attempt to appeal to everyone for your website. But as we've always discovered with our lovely host from Boostly, that's probably not the best idea.

So in this case, simply knock-up two websites.

For example, one for leisure guests and one for contractors. It sounds simple enough, right?

Just buy two domains.

One with your main business name. The other, referring to your location and who you're speaking to.

Scarboroughcontractorstays, for example.

We will talk about your website later in the book. For now, go and do the task.

If your website needs changing, tell me what you're going to do via Instagram: @boostlyuk

And then come back to continue with the next part of the content.

In the final part of this chapter we will ensure that your guest experience is spot on, every time.

THE
BOOK DIRECT
PLAYBOOK

SETTING UP YOUR PROPERTY, PROPERLY

This part of the chapter is so key, but so many ignore it.

Please don't make the (common) mistake of skipping this chapter. This is your heads up: the content in this section is **absolutely key.**

To help me put my point across, I'm going to take you back to a trip I took in 2019.

Laura and our three boys wanted to get away for a few days. We'd actually just moved to Spain at this point, and were in the process of getting the boys into a good Spanish school.

So, with a few weeks free in between, our travel-heads thought why not go out and explore for a bit?

Pretty soon, we found an ideal-looking place and proceeded to book directly. We also messaged the host beforehand to let him know that we had a baby, plus two children under the age of seven.

The host replied 'No problem.'

Everything seemed fine and dandy so far. In fact, the property had even advertised 'super fast Wifi', which is a must for me and my business.

Anyway, it was a long drive up the coast. By the time we arrived at the property, we were looking forward to crashing down with a carb-loaded takeaway and getting the boys into bed.

Upon first impressions, the property looked lovely. It was a great location (as aptly advertised), close to the sea, and the host personally greeted us and showed us in.

Everything seemed perfect enough.

Now, before I continue on with my story - and I really must interject that in hospitality, your business lives and dies on one key factor:

The reviews.

If a guest has a good experience they tell 2 people about you instantly.

If a guest has a bad experience they tell the whole world!

As the saying goes, first impressions are everything. You truly never do get a second chance to make a first impression.

In fact, I'll even go as far as elaborating that a few poor reviews on OTAs and your property will vanish from the first page of their SEO listings. And of course, guests are far quicker at leaving negative reviews as opposed to positive ones (especially if they're really miffed off). So, the best way you can avoid this completely, is by setting up your property in the right way.

Anyway, keep that in mind while I return to my story:

So, if you're a parent then you'll relate to this - but when you first check into a short-term rental property with children, the first thing you do is check for 'baby proofing' (i.e., ensure that the accommodation is safe for babies and toddlers, alike).

But in a property that was clearly advertised as 'family friendly' - which is why we booked it - I ended up spending thirty minutes baby proofing it myself, upon check-in. I mean, it was packed to the corners with breakable furniture, and dangerous ornaments scattered left, right, and centre.

It was a ginormous accident waiting to happen. Everything within hand's reach of my excitable one-year old.

As for the 'super fast Wifi', unfortunately, that was anything but. I'd say about 10mbps download, or less - and the upload speed was absolutely abysmal.

Now you see - setting your guest's expectation is everything. It's shocking how many professionals forget this in hospitality.

There's a very fine balance between under promising and over delivering, and over promising and under delivering (and thus, attracting poor reviews). Over a period of time, this becomes the difference between a successful and a sinking hospitality business.

The property which we stayed at in Spain was fine. Though it didn't deliver upon our expectations (and yes, we were left disappointed).

As hospitality professionals and a family who has travelled the world several times over, we didn't leave a scathing review about the host and their accommodation. I guess that's the soft spot within all us hospitality folk.

However, I did leave a quick message saying the following: **'Hey, so maybe don't leave the breakables out for 1 year olds and the wifi speed isn't as advertised.'** And I truly hope that the host took heed of this, for the benefit of his own business.

Needless to say, if we're ever in that part of Spain again, looking for a place to crash with the family, it's unlikely that we'll return to this accommodation. And that's precisely my point, see?

A failure to set up your property correctly for your ideal guests won't just cost you good reviews, but it'll also cost you repeat custom - which is what short-term rental businesses need to survive.

Had this property host decluttered their living room area, or organised a better Broadband provider, the story would have been quite different. Ultimately, it's all about implementing the steps outlined in the first section of this Playbook (and I'd advise you to flip back to it, if you haven't covered it already), to ensure that you're guaranteeing a positive guest experience.

Preparation is excellent. But it's the final delivery that makes a difference **- remember that, squad.**

GET IT DONE

If you can, go and have a nosey around your property; or better still stay there for a few days.

Stay there with your ideal guest firmly in mind.

It may be strange, and you may lose a few nights' income but in the long term, it will help you understand your service offering better (and we all deserve to treat ourselves now and again).

Put yourself in your guests' shoes.

THE HIGHLIGHTS

You've certainly shown your champion's spirit till this point of the Playbook! What an epic start it's been; we've ticked off some vital short-term rental learnings and introduced the idea of 'There's a Story Behind Every Booking'.

I've purposely loaded it with plenty of **Get it Done** sessions. Mainly because the Customer Avator section for me, is one of the most important things to nail for your business.

You need to know exactly who it is you're serving. Otherwise, you'll just be creating blindly and 'hoping' for the best.

So, let this be your biggest takeaway so far: **Get crystal clear on who your ideal guest is.**

Remember, as we've already covered, it's okay to have more than one customer avatar. For this, I'd recommend following that golden **80/20 rule**. (What 20% of attributes align with your guests, 80% of the time).

Once you figure out who your people are, I promise you, life will get a lot easier.

I'm going to finish off this section with another powerful quote now. Memorise it like a mantra:

WHEN YOU APPEAL TO EVERYONE, YOU APPEAL TO NO ONE.

Right, I'm going to squeeze in one more section into the **First Half** of this Playbook, because it perfectly aligns with what we've already covered.

If you've skipped ahead to this section, then the majority of tips here will still make sense. But be sure to flip back and read about your ideal guest, when you get the chance. That'll really help you maximise on the benefits of what's to come (and what's to come is truly exciting!).

So, just to refresh your memory in Chapters 1 and 2, we have heavily focused on laying the foundation for every successful hospitality business.

Now, to the next bit.

Getting into it requires a bit of nostalgia (the tangent will be worth it, I promise).

One of my favourite lessons I learned at school was about stone bridges.

I always remember this lesson from my primary school teacher. We learned about how there's a key component to building a stone bridge.

It wasn't at the start, or at the end; but in fact, in the middle.

It's called The Keystone and this ensures that the bridge doesn't fall down nor collapse

Without the keystone, the bridge would fail to remain secure. This feature is prevalent and stands out massively every time you look at a stone bridge.

In the same way, when it comes to the keystone in your business, it is of course your direct bookings website.

YOUR WEBSITE IS 'THE KEYSTONE'

There's no point in going ahead with getting all your systems in place and then doing all the marketing, if you haven't even got a website that works. This is pretty obvious.

The trouble is, people overcomplicate websites and while this would make perfect sense if you were building a multi-functional E-Commerce platform, it certainly doesn't have to be the case with a book direct website.

But once again, I come bearing good news! I'm going to give you the exact layout and structure that we use at our website agency, so you can put it into practice straight away. Let me tell you, these babies work - and you don't need to be a tech guru to understand what I'm about to cover.

THIS CHAPTER OUT OF THE ENTIRE BOOK, SHOULD BE A MUST!

I can already envision while I'm writing this book, that when I come to do the interviews to promote it and the interviewer asks me:

"Which chapter in the Playbook should everyone read?"

And my answer will be, **this one.**

Some of the points I'll talk about will need visual aids, so for that I've added tutorial videos to the companion course to this book which is at bookdirectplaybook.com.

What you are going to learn are the key components to every website.

This is based on years of research, consuming hundreds of surveys, keeping on track with all the latest blogs and Google updates and most importantly, testing it on thousands of other hosts and their websites that we have designed over the years.

To be honest, this chapter could be a book within itself, so I'm going to make sure that I keep the sections short and encourage everyone to delve over to the companion course to get the more detailed over the shoulder look.

The course will also share tools that we use as a company, which have been our 'secret sauce' up to now.

There will be mini Get It Done sessions in this chapter, but it is up to you if you consume it all in one go and then complete them after, or simply work on them while getting through this chapter.

Ready for the must-see action? **Let's play ball!**

WHICH CMS TO USE?

Firstly, what is a CMS? Well, the internet tells us this:

A content management system or CMS is a software that is used to build websites and create content to be published on the internet. Typically CMS allows you to create a website without writing any code.

In a nutshell, there are several types of CMS providers.

1 | The one your PMS gives you, for free

2 | Wix

3 | Squarespace

4 | Weebly

5 | Wordpress

Now, we could have a big old debate about which one to use, but we would be here for hours on end.

The PMS providers will all tell you that theirs is the best because, to put it frankly, they want your business.

There will be some people who swear by Wix, Squarespace or Weebly, and I say this with the biggest smile on my face:

They don't know what they are talking about.

I want to make sure this section is as short as possible, so we can get into the juicy stuff.

Trust me when I say this, and I have reviewed over 100 websites, studied countless courses, surveys, webinars, invested time with the experts of SEO and much more: **Wordpress is the only CMS to use.**

There is a reason why in 2020 38% of the world's websites were powered by Wordpress. A number that will have only increased by the time you're consuming this book.

There is a reason why we build our Boostly websites on Wordpress.

They simply work the best.

They're powerful and most versatile when it comes to the number of tools we can add on and use. And hey, I'm going to throw a real technical term your way now:

They're **Open Source**, which means that Google prefers it for SEO related purposes than any other option.

Now, if you're one of the people who swears by another option; I may have hit a nerve.

I would love for you to reach out to me via Instagram or email: mark@ boostly.co.uk and put an argument as to why. We're always tolerant of a difference in opinion here.

But I should warn you, I've been part of numerous discussions, many posts in online groups, as well as webinars about this topic and I am yet to hear a convincing enough argument that will persuade me otherwise. I say this with the greatest respect.

If your website is not currently built on Wordpress, then I encourage you ASAP to change it.

If you want recommendations, then please send me a message on Instagram @boostlyuk or email info@boostly.co.uk and I will be sure to help and assist.

MOBILE-FIRST WEBSITES

Okay, let's dig into the juicy bits.

In this chapter I'm going to explain to you all the key aspects of your website and what to implement today. Right here, right now.

I would love for you to take a before and after picture of your website and send it to me via Instagram or tag me in a post, because this is going to be so, so powerful.

I'm going to share with you countless hours of study, thousands of pounds invested in courses and lots of success stories from #teamboostly members. We'll also cover a lot of topics; but I'm going to start with the one mentioned in the above title first (because I believe it to be the most important).

When you come to designing your website, you need to make sure it's built for mobile phones first. Take a moment to consider how many people spend their entire lifetimes on their mobile phones, and you'll see where I'm coming from.

So, you may be wondering what designing a website for mobile phones even means?

In a nutshell, it basically refers to the styling, the layout, the text size, and the features of your respective website - **as experienced on a mobile phone screen.**

And just to make it really clear, the reason why we're giving mobile websites so much importance is because..

In a recent study, in October 2020, there were 4.6B people accessing the internet, 91% of them accessed the internet via their mobile device.

Mobile is the most popular channel.

But here is the problem.

Website designers and hosts, to this day, build out their mobile on a desktop and in desktop view.

Which is ironic (and wrong), because the guest experience is everything. It's about:

- How you communicate with guests, pre-stay

- How their experience is in your property, during the time of stay

- How you communication with guests, post stay

Every step matters.

The most important part is right at the beginning. Before the guests even decide to book with you.

At this point, guest experience on your website could be the deciding factor between whether they book directly with you, or with someone else.

Or worse, whether they use a third party and book with you via them, because their 'experience' is better.

We have been building mobile first websites since 2018, at Boostly and it's a core contributor in turning 'Lookers into Bookers'. Checking if a website is mobile-friendly is actually very easy. And I'm going to show you exactly how.

GET IT DONE

Get your phone out, and load up your website.

And run through a 'dummy booking'.

Go through the whole process.

If you feel you're too biased, get a friend or family member to do it for you.

If you don't trust them to be brutally honest, go to usertesting.com (we've already used this in an earlier part of the Playbook). But for a very decent rate, you can hire people to test your website from a guest perspective.

Whenever we launch a new template or website, we do this and have done for years.

It's invaluable.

What are you looking for?

- Can you click on the buttons okay?

- Do you have to pinch the screen to zoom in to see text?

- Is it clear where to make a booking?

- Is it simple to make a payment and book a stay?

If you answered 'no' to any of the above questions, then it's time for you to do something about it.

If you want to see these types in action, then head to bookdirectplaybook.com and access the video.

YOUR HOMEPAGE

When a guest visits your website homepage, it is akin to them walking through the front door of your accommodation for the first time.

This is the best way to approach it. I've never understood why people in our industry over-intellectualise the mechanics of a website homepage, or worse, try to make it look like the next Mona Lisa.

The secret to a hospitality business's website (and I know this after studying some of the best websites, representing some of the biggest chains in our industry) is...simplicity.

Simplicity.

A concept lost on many people; especially as the market becomes increasingly competitive. But here's the thing: simple does not mean boring.

Nor does simple mean 'basic', 'easy', or lacking any kind of substance. In fact, simplicity is the exact opposite of all these things - just ask a copywriter, and they'll tell you exactly why.

Please understand that the purpose of a hospitality website - and the homepage in particular - is to drive people from the website to the glorified direct booking engine. That's where all the action happens; and that's where you need to aid your website visitors to land on, **and fast.**

Time really is of the essence when it comes to home pages, and I'm sure you've heard this several times. But if a potential guest lands on your website homepage and is left feeling confused or overwhelmed within the first few seconds, then you can sure-bet that they'll leave.

They'll press that little 'x' button on the top left-hand corner of their screen and they won't return.

So, just to make it super-clear squad: **First Impressions Count.**

We've all learned these humble lessons in school about 'not judging a book by its cover' and that's all wonderful. But in this arena of business, people are going to judge you - and they're going to judge you hard.

Anyway, as you know I'm a solution based kinda' guy. So, in this section of the Playbook, I'm going to lay out exactly what you need to do, in order to create an epic homepage that guests will want to hang around on.

We'll take it step-by-step; no prior (technical) knowledge needed. But it'd be worth checking out the **Customer Avator** section, if you haven't already.

ABOVE THE FOLD

For a video-version of this chapter, where you get to see actual examples and a cool walk through of the details, head on over to: bookdirectplaybook.com

Now, before we continue, I want to state the obvious.

When you're thinking about this section and the changes you're going to make on your website homepage, be sure to have one thing in mind.

'How will this look on a mobile device?'

When your website loads, there is something the techie geeks like to refer to as **'above the fold'.**

This is just a smart way of describing the first bit of content Future Potential Guests (FPGs) see, as soon as they land on your homepage without having to scroll down.

Simply put, it's the deciding factor on whether they'd like to stay or leave your website. So, it's important stuff.

Going back to my point about 'time', statistics tell us that you have just 8 seconds to explain who you clearly are to website visitors, as well as what services your business provides, and how you can benefit your FPG from the moment they land on your homepage.

8 seconds.

And that time will only decrease.

In a world of instant gratification, with the likes of Netflix, YouTube, Amazon Prime, and instant booking with Booking.com, Airbnb and suchlike, we have been conditioned to be extreeeeemely impatient!

Just the other day, I saw a friend of mine complain about their Uber taking more than five minutes to arrive (and yes, they posted this instantly, on social media).

Now, as mentioned earlier, you'll need to crack Chapter Two of this Playbook to get the most out of this section. So, if you haven't clearly identified WHO it is you're speaking to on your website, it's best to flip back a few pages, and figure this out first. Trust me, it'll be worth the extra time you put in.

Once you've seen to the above, you need to ensure that you do these three crucial things, when looking at your homepage's above the fold section:

1 | Use the best possible image to promote your business

2 | Capture your ideal guest with a headline based on *their needs*

3 | Have a clear call-to-action button where they can book directly

GET IT DONE

This is a great little exercise to get you thinking about the above the fold section.

So, first of all, grab your phone and show it to a stranger. This stranger cannot be a family member or friend who already knows what you do, business wise.

If you're sitting in a coffee shop right now, go ahead and ask the person who's sitting at the table next to you.

Show this lovely person your phone and load up your website; then ask them:

'Can you please tell me what you think this website is all about?'

Now, you MUST only show the stranger your website for five seconds, that's the only way you'll get an accurate response.

If, after the five seconds, the stranger cannot explain:

1 | What your website is about

2 | Who your business helps

3 | How guests can book with you

Then you have failed in your mission to keep things simple.

This neat little test was initially described to me as the '7 year-old test' and I was very fortunate to have a 7 year-old at the time to perform this test.

However, his response was:

'Leave me alone, Daddy.'

So, I have since rebranded this to the 'stranger test' - and it still works just as well. Give it a try for yourself and let me know how you got on.

If afterwards, you fancy taking a look at excellent examples of above the fold layouts, head on over to: boostly.co.uk/portfolio - there are hundreds of examples right there, for you to get inspired by.

ICONS > TEXT

As an author who is writing a book, this may be about the most banal thing ever.

People don't read.

They skim read at most.

Now I know this sounds ridiculous, but it is true (notice the short paragraphs in this Playbook, they're here for a reason).

And the same is true of your website.

Please, whatever you do, do not put big blocks of text on your website. There is nothing more off-putting.

People do not read them.

And to all my SEO friends who'll argue that masses of content is great for SEO (which it is), please remember that this detail-rich content is better placed elsewhere on your website - and certainly not on your homepage, and where you expect guests to take immediate action.

During my research for this section of the Playbook (and while we were working on some of our latest Boostly website designs), I came across this:

SUCCESS LEAVES CLUES

You see, I wanted to see what the Online Travel Agents were doing on their website, as well what the big hotel chains were implementing into their marketing and digital set-ups.

Of course, these colossal companies are fortunate enough to hire teams of people to test every single button, text, copy, layout, for every section of their website and app. They easily spend millions in research and implementing their design - even if it's something as intricate as reducing size 14 font to size 12.

But I compiled all my research for free. I simply took what the top 10 companies in the world of hospitality were doing, found the most common factors and hey presto, implemented it into Boostly.

SUCCESS LEAVES CLUES

In my research, I noticed that instead of using big blocks of text, these big hospitality companies were using icons, particularly to pinpoint main features and amenities.

It's genius really.

Now, there's no way you can instantly tell me the answer to this...

But I expect that you'll nod your head in silence, and agree...

Pull out your phone and look at the last few text messages you've sent - to family, friends, or otherwise.

What's the first thing you notice in your text messages?

Emojis.

Emojis are taking over our lives.

I barely send a message without one. It's about as frequent as a full stop.

It's funny, we're going full circle as the human race. From the early form of ancient Egyptians communicating via hieroglyphics; and now in a world where emojis seem to be the universal language, across all age groups, genders, and creeds.

Without going too far on a tangent, this makes sense as to why icons are so popular on hospitality websites.

You can easily put a shower icon and someone will recognise that this room has a shower.

You can add an icon of a family and it will clearly insinuate 'family friendly'.

Of course, I'm not saying that your entire website should be jam-packed with icons. Going back to my earlier point, remember that simplicity is crucial here.

Less is more.

However, the home page is where you need to use as few words as possible. Which is actually a skill within itself.

The FPG is going to be skim reading, so make sure you don't overwhelm them with choices, nor the decisions they need to make.

A PHOTO TELLS A 1000 WORDS

I will talk more about photos later in this book, but I can't stress this enough.

The first impressions of your property and the likelihood of potential booking, lays hugely on the standard of your photographs.

Take my word on this one as I am speaking from experience.

Do not skimp on the cost of your photos.

A poorly lit photo could be the deciding factor between a big booking or not. For years, my Dad would take out his old camera and walk round around the property in our family business and say:

'This will do.'

And then pass me the camera.

Honestly, it's amazing that we ever got any bookings. I swear in some of the photos, the bed wasn't even made! Makes me cringe when I think about it now.

You might be lucky like me, as I had a friend who was a professional photographer.

Not only a professional photographer, but he specialised in interior photoshoots.

This is the key here, you need to find someone who is an expert not only with photography, but interior photography. (Not every photographer will capture the nuances of your renovated kitchens).

I understand that when you're starting out in business, the budget is scarce - if not non-existent - which is precisely why I've created a video that'll help you find a professional photographer for free, or at a very low cost.

Find the video on the companion course of this at bookdirectplaybook. com

Once you have your professional photos, placement on the website is key.

You'll need to treat your homepage as if the guest is telling themselves a story as they are scrolling down. Remember, people are far more likely to stay engaged if they feel part of a story - and this stuff has been scientifically backed and proven.

Unbeknown to many of them, guests will have a mental checklist to cross off in their heads as they're navigating through your website. So, how you say you're going to help them is key.

If you address the points on their mental checklist in their wrong order on your website homepage, you will confuse them (and in-turn, lose them).

That is exactly why you need to showcase your rooms or your property portfolio high up on your website. It needs to be one of the first things the FPG sees.

So, ideally, right beneath the above the fold section of the page.

You should be showcasing your business with the best images possible.

Unique Selling Photos

... as I like to call them.

The entire point here is to get the user to click to **find out more,** or book their stay.

CLEAR CALL TO ACTION

A call-to-action button is the specific button the FPG will click to find out more.

Usually, you will take the potential guest to your booking page, to a phone call, or email, or to search for more information on your website.

Many people make the mistake of having a call to action button at the top of their website, and nowhere else. This includes numerous website designers who won't always understand the journey your FPG is on.

Think of the guest experience.

If you have a potential guest scrolling down your page (which of course, you WANT them to do), the last thing you'll then do is have no other CTA button further down the website. It makes no sense. It's extra work for your website visitor and it gives the impression that you don't believe in your business and aren't too bothered whether guests book with you or not.

Of course, there's a fine balance between not having any CTA buttons and getting trigger-happy with it.

The best way to strike this balance is to include a CTA button after each respective section of your website homepage. You can refer back to the video explanation on the bookdirectplaybook.com for a visual example of this (I highly recommend that you do).

Also consider that the most important thing about your CTA buttons is that they need to stand out.

It needs to be crystal-clear to the FPG what is going to happen, after they click on that magic button.

So, go ahead and use a different, striking colour for your CTA buttons. Try and keep it on-brand, but also different from all the other text and images surrounding it.

Another quick-fix is to type the text in capital letters and maybe even format it in bold. Add an exclamation point if you need to (!) but don't go overboard and start 'shouting' at your guests.

The easiest way for this is to have it a different colour from everything else that is around it.

High conversion words in our industry include:

BOOK NOW

BOOK A FREE CALL

CHECK AVAILABILITY

ENQUIRE HERE

CALL US, NOW

START YOUR BOOKING PROCESS

FIND OUT MORE

As a bonus point, let me tell you that where you can squeeze the word 'you' into your CTA button text, definitely do it. Website visitors love being spoken to directly, and are far more likely to have a (positive) emotional reaction to your copy.

ABOUT YOU

A few years back I was hosting a live call. I'm actually going to tell you all about this encounter, as it hits home an extremely important point.

Plus **'There's a Story Behind Every Booking',** remember?

So, during this live call, I encouraged the property hosts on the call with me to come up and ask questions, and share their frustration when it came to marketing.

We had over 100 people on the call and I will never forget a conversation with this one particular host.

She lived in a busy coastal town in the UK.

She was doubting herself and how her business would stand out.

I want to share with you the advice I gave to her, because it's not uncommon for a host to get themselves into a worry thanks to self doubt and that dreaded 'imposter syndrome'. However, these things are the enemies of your growth, and need to be tackled, head on.

The advice I offered, went something like this:

> 'There are hundreds of other hospitality businesses in your area.
>
> The street you're located on, there must be another 30 at least...
>
> You could all have the same bedding, the same wallpaper, the same furniture. Even your breakfasts may be carbon copies of each other.
>
> But, the one thing that separates you from everyone else is what nobody else can ever replicate...
>
> And that is YOU.
>
> Your personality, your story, how you interact with your guests.
>
> No one can replicate you.
>
> There's only one of you.
>
> People buy from people.

Consider for a second, what an absolutely bizarre people-focused industry we're all in.

We basically invite strangers to live in our houses.

We can't help but be people-focused.

This is why it is so important on your website that you share your unique story.

The simplest way to do this is in your **About Us** section - and then you can repurpose it across different platforms, if you want.

It doesn't have to be a novel. In fact, it probably shouldn't be.

Just a paragraph or two, introducing you, your family, your pet dogs, and your valued team.

Share some photos.

People love to know who they're going to be staying with. Even if you don't live on-site, this stuff makes a difference.

Now, you may love or hate a selfie or photos being taken of you; but it needs to be done.

So smile, and take a photo.

And use it.

EXPLAIN THE PROCESS

Far too often, the reason why a FPG leaves your website is because they're confused.

They're confused about how to give you money; and they don't have the time to hang around, crack some kind of morse code, and figure it out.

The problem is, you'll unintentionally make your website so confusing, to the point where FPGs don't even know where to go to book. It's leaving cold, hard money on the table. (And it's not the best move, on your part).

This is why you need to have a clear section laid out on your website explaining in ideally **3 steps** how the potential guest can book.

Bish. Bash. Bosh.

It needs to be in as few words as possible.

And of course, using icons for this always helps.

For another real-life example, check out boostly.co.uk/portfolio

But here's one for you below, as I'm in a generous mood:

1 | Check dates and availability for your chosen room/ property

2 | Fill in the form and tell us about you and your travelling party

3 | Complete the booking with our secure checkout process

With this, the FPG has no doubt in their mind on what they need to do.

If you really want to take things up a notch you could also record a quick video showing the guest the booking process. The bravest reap the biggest rewards.

We said a photo can speak a 1000 words.

Well a video speaks a million.

A video shows the user exactly what to do - and will appeal to a much larger demographic.

Sometimes by simply showing the process, you can set the difference between a direct booking taking place, or not.

REVIEWS

The final two subsections of this part of the book are my secret sauce. The bit that loads of other people forget, or simply don't think of. This is potentially costing them thousands in bookings.

One of my favourite books is *Influence* by Robert Ciadini. In there is a quote: 'we view a behavior as more correct in a given situation to the degree that we see others performing it.'

92% of people only buy a product or
make a decision after reading reviews.

Having real reviews on your website is a game-changer.

So, it begs the question, why aren't you doing it?

Or even worse, why oh why must you copy and paste reviews (come on, I know some of you do).

With respect...

They look fake.

There are plenty of review tools now that you can join and simply link to your social platforms, Google reviews, and more. Once you've done that you can place them on your website and they update in realtime.

You can even set filters where only your 5 star reviews will be in public viewing.

If you would like to get a list of recommended companies to use, go and check out the resources section on bookdirectplaybook.com. Even if there's just one thing you take away from this chapter and implement, please let it be this.

This is something you can do today. And the rewards will be immense.

FAQs

My final bit of secret sauce in this section is the Frequently Asked Questions.

Not only is this a fantastic checklist exercise for your FPG, but Google ranks websites much, much higher if they have a correctly laid out FAQ page. Also, remember when we mentioned more text for the purpose of SEO? Yes, this ticks that box, too.

The good news is that there are plenty of tools and plugins that you can add to your website for you to implement here.

If you're struggling to think of what your FAQs could be, a really useful tip is to open up your emails and search all your guest questions that have landed in your inbox over the past year.

Read through them all and make a note of the 20% of questions that come up 80% of the time. We introduce the 80/20 over on Chapter One (check it out).

And there are your FAQs.

Not random questions that you've come up with, off the top of your head. But questions that your ideal guests are actually asking.

You should be placing your FAQs at the bottom of your home page. This leaves room for your menu and any other pages that you have not shown the FPG.

Don't forget to have a good CTA button and also leave some links to your social media channels.

Guests love to interact with hospitality businesses online - this is something I'll cover in a later section of this Playbook.

LIVE CHAT TOOL

A massively underestimated free tool that doesn't get used enough for hospitality websites is **live chat.**

There are many plugins out there and as with anything in life, they each have their own pros and cons.

I believe the reason why Live Chat Tools don't get incorporated onto hospitality websites a lot of the time, is because of the name. The term 'live chat' kind of makes you feel as though you need to be online 24/7, which is exhausting to even think about.

What if I said that a study showed that 76% of travellers said that they would contact the property they

were trying to book at if they had a
question at the point of booking.

The tools that are available now mean that you don't need to be online all the time.

You can set your times so that when you're away, guests can easily use the tool to get in touch. The Live Chat tool could automatically respond with an FAQ answer, or you can enter key phrases for the most popular questions and the guest would again get an instant, automated reply.

Another reason why I believe so many website designers don't add it in for you is because they don't look 'nice'.

I should reiterate, we're not creating the next Mona Lisa here.

We're creating a website that has one core goal:

To turn a looker into a booker.

For a list of resources and tools for Live Chat, I recommend that you hop on over to: bookdirectplaybook.com

LEAD GENERATION TOOLS

I'm going to let you into a 'behind the scenes' secret of the planning of this very Playbook. I was actually going to title this section 'Pop Ups'.

Do you want to know why I changed my mind?

Well, I knew that some people would skirt over it if I did.

Pop-ups have such a bad reputation in our world. Often known for being those annoying flashy boxes that have the tiniest little 'x' button placed on them (and annoying website visitors even more).

People associate them with spammy websites that are trying to rip you off.

And I know this for a fact because we've built over 1000 websites at Boostly and every time we recommend hosts to have a lead generation tool, we're always faced with hesitation or point-blank refusal.

The thing is, these pop-ups can be annoying at the best of times - but guess what? They absolutely work!

Now, I'm not for one minute recommending that you go off and shove pop up boxes all over your direct bookings website. However, what you do need to do here is think differently and change that mindset.

For once in your life, I want you to think *inside* the box (and yes, pun totally intended).

The main reason why people make the most of pop ups and lead generation tools for their website, is because they know that the chances of a user (who's never heard of your business before) converting from a 'looker' into a 'booker' are slim.

There's two terms I use here:

The **Slow Lane** and the **Fast Lane.**

Think back to the last journey you went on.

You have destination A and destination B.

For this example, let's have A as the Looker and B as the Booker.

Your goal with promoting your business (and this is what the OTAs do so well) is to get the Future Potential Guest (FPG, remember) from A to B as quickly as possible.

With me so far?

Great.

So, the longer it takes you to get them from A to B, the greater the chances of them becoming distracted, or worse, completely uninterested.

With this in mind, the 'Slow Lane' includes the following types of actions:

- ▪ Someone liking your post on social media

- ▪ Someone seeing your advert and listing online

- Someone watching your video

- Someone visiting your website

This is all stuff in the slow lane. Slow as a cup of Joe in a crowded Starbucks.

The slow lane can seem all well and good; and yes, it might lead guests to getting to their destination on time. However, there's also a big chance of them getting distracted or losing interest, thus, settling with a new destination altogether.

So, the goal has got to be to get FPGs into the Fast Lane of your funnel.

I believe in this theory so passionately. In fact, so much so that I'm going to dedicate an entire chapter to it.

It's had such a massive positive impact on my businesses over the years and of all of the tactics and training I teach hosts globally, the one that has the best results (and costs zero money) is email marketing. A great strategy for getting into the Fast Lane.

But, I'm getting ahead of myself here. Don't worry, we'll explore the nooks and crannies of email marketing later on in this Playbook.

For now, I want you to stay thinking about your website.

Ask yourself, where can you on your home page (or website as a whole) add in a lead generation section?

You'll be happy to know that this doesn't have to be a pop-up.

It can be a nicely placed call-to-action button.

Because, hot news! Not every CTA button has to be a prompt and get the guest to book now. There's a whole bunch of other things you can get your FPG to do during their direct bookings journey.

Don't forget that in the booking process, the FPG might be at the planning stage and is not ready to move to the deciding stage - so, you've got to cover all grounds and not jump into the selling bit too soon.

This is why a nicely-timed, lead generation tool could work wonders in transporting guests from the Slow Lane to the hyper-cool Fast Lane. As always, there are tools out there which will help you with this and lucky for you, they're all placed in the **Resources Section** on bookdirectplaybook.com.

In terms of the text to have on this lead generation tool...

Something like:

Join My Newsletter

Doesn't have quite the same appeal as:

Discover the Top 4 Places to Visit in [insert your town]

Try these 3 Quick & Easy Home Recipes, Guaranteed to Wow Your Guests

The trick here is to hook your lead generation message to the desires and needs of your customer avatar, rather than just making it about yourself. If you've skipped the chapter on this then flip back to it and delve in.

Then come back here and give it your best shot.

Right now, you may be wondering, how do I get someone from my website to my email list?

Again, that will be covered in the later chapter.

All I want for you to do in this section is to **change your mindset** on this topic. Everything else will come later.

If you want to check out a subtle yet wickedly effective lead generation tool in place, then visit boostly.co.uk

Give me your honest thoughts on whether you think it's helpful, intrusive, or just plain annoying - by sending me a DM on Instagram, at @boostlyuk

TO BLOG OR NOT TO BLOG?

... that is the question.

And a common one at that, especially in my hospitality Facebook group.

Stuff like:

'Do I need to blog?'

or

'How do I rank better in the Search Engines?'

Always pops up.

We'll focus more on the latter, later. But to answer the first question (bluntly): **yes.** However, while we're here, I should tell you that blogging will help you with that second question, too.

Blogs on your website do two main things:

1 | Updates the search engines and tells platforms that you have fresh content on your website. Which is what they want, bingo!

2 | Helps your business and website stand out from the rest

Let's focus on point number two, for now. When we build a website, we have a structure, a layout, and a wireframe that works every time.

This is why we never custom build for someone.

We know what works from reviewing, testing and launching thousands of other hospitality websites.

A negative dig by a competitor (who will remain nameless) was that:

'Boostly websites all look the same.'

And my reply, with of course, the biggest smile on my face, was:

'If they work, then is it such a bad thing?'

In fact, this is exactly why I've introduced a money back guarantee that refunds 100% of a host's money if they don't see return on investment in new direct bookings.

As I have stated in this Playbook already...

You can have an entire street of hospitality businesses.

All of them with the same decor, the same beds, and the same scenic views.

What sets each of them apart is you, the host.

You need to stamp your personality all over it.

And so, blogging is a fantastic way to do this.

But before you go tapping away at your computer, please remember to only write and publish content that is of actual value to your ideal guest. You need to have a clear idea of your customer avatar and only then will you be able to create great content for them (otherwise, you're wasting your time).

If you're looking to appeal to young families, you're not going to write about the best places to go for a drink after 11 pm on your website. That's going to do more harm to your business than good.

Please remember, squad, I'm not saying for one second that you need to be blogging every day. I get that it's time consuming, and probably a bigger challenge for some, than others. But if you can look to put something together once a quarter at least (and this way, it'll be manageable to outsource, if you need), then you're going to be doing 80% more than your local competitors.

THE
BOOK DIRECT
PLAYBOOK

THE DOMAIN NAME

W hy do people stress out about this topic more than any other?

Why do people relentlessly believe that what your domain is, has any impact on how highly you rank in the search engines?

I'm addressing these points because I come across them most in our support emails. Hosts postponing the 'Go Live' date of their websites because they haven't found the perfect domain. It's so shockingly common.

My advice on this is that as long as your domain name is short and easy to type on a mobile device, you're on to a winner. For bonus points, try and make it memorable and easy to spell and pronounce as well. This is not the time to be the next William Shakespeare.

You've got to take my word for it here. We actually had this issue back at my family business for years! Now's a great time to dive into another short story.

THERE'S A STORY BEHIND EVERY BOOKING.

So, the story is that (as you know) our family business is called The Grainary. And as you'd expect, the domain was: grainary.co.uk. But over the years, the number of incorrect spelling variations that we came across was insane!

Granary

Grainery

Granairy

The list goes on.

I know for a fact that The Granary Cottages, which were based about two hours from us in Yorkshire, received heaps of business from guests who thought they were booking into *our* short-stay accommodation, but couldn't get the spelling right. You wouldn't believe the number of times we'd receive their reviews on our TripAdvisor page, saying: **'It wasn't what I was expecting!'**

What a ginormous mix-up, all in the name of a few consonants.

Please. Learn from our mistakes.

Pick a domain (and business) name that is easy to spell.

Furthermore, let this be your takeaway here...

YOU SHOULD HAVE MULTIPLE WEBSITES

I know what you're thinking:

MULTIPLE WEBSITES?!

This is important, so hear me out. (Or read on, you know what I mean)...

You'll remember from earlier in this chapter I spoke about 'above the fold', i.e. that all-important first impression. How we only have 8 short seconds to clearly explain to the potential future guest who we are, who we help, and how to book.

Also, in the customer avatar chapter I explained that we might have a situation where we want to appeal to a few different types of guests.

THE DOMAIN NAME 101

Do you remember? If not, then quickly flip back to that part of the Playbook.

So, if this is the case for you and you're speaking to more than one audience, then adopting the idea of multiple websites could make life a heck of a lot easier for you.

Because, you CAN'T cram everything onto one website.

You can't create a compelling headline and tagline if you're trying to appeal to more than one avatar. Trust me, I tried and failed miserably with Boostly.

Which is why I decided to break the Boostly 'umbrella' down into four sub-brands.

Boostly Content Creator

Boostly Academy

Boostly Website Design

Boostly Podcast

Initially, I was trying to squeeze everything into the main domain, boostly.co.uk.

The problem with this was that if we had a potential customer who was visiting us online to enquire about website design, they would end up landing on the website's main homepage, which ushered them to join Boostly's email list.

The host would quickly become frustrated because we wouldn't serve their immediate need and as a result, we lost.

So, I came up with the idea of categorising the Boostly website. Creating a neat 'box' for each division of the business - which makes me sound incredibly 'adult'.

Now, I can't even begin to explain how much this boosted business and made it sooo much easier for me to monitor which bit of custom was coming from where. It was like my business was this giant slapdash kitchen and somebody had come in to fit some lovely cabinets, drawers, and table tops into it.

In fact, this new change of approach worked so well for Boostly that we enthusiastically introduced it to our website clients, who had different brands within their one business.

And as I'd positively anticipated, it worked a treat for them, too.

This included hosts who had a large leisure market, but also wanted to fill their mid-week calendar with business guests. As well as hosts who wanted to attract wedding couples and run a corporate hospitality business during the right seasons.

It was a winning game plan. Every single time.

I know it sounds like a lot of 'extra work'. And I'm not here to make your life more complicated and rob you of all your evenings and weekends But remember this, your main website is a (digital) pillar of your entire hospitality business - probably the one that carries the most weight. It is the one place where all the need-to-knows about your business will be, so it's certainly worth the extra effort. Plus, once you've sorted the initial structure out, the rest will fall into place a lot faster.

So, after you've created an epic homepage and structure for your main website (the one that will represent all your sub-brands and divisions), you simply need to create a one-page website for all the other parts of your business. Just like we've done for Boostly.

As a point of reference, if you head over to Boostly's website page now, (boostlywebsite.com) you'll see that it's a straightforward one-page website, with all the details you need about that particular product.

But if you were to visit the main domain (boostly.co.uk), you'll notice a big difference in layout, content and depth of detail. That's because we're speaking to a completely different audience there.

It's an easy enough tactic to get your head around; but don't underestimate it because of its simplicity. When executed correctly, this one change will have the potential to make a lasting impact on your hospitality business...for the better.

TEST, TEST, AND TEST SOME MORE

Congratulations! If you're working through this Playbook in order, then you now have websites and they are LIVE.

So, now you need to test them.

It's vital that you know how many people are visiting your website(s), as well as which sections of the website they're warming to most, how long they stick around on said website section, and, of course, how many of them click on your perfectly crafted CTA buttons.

Identifying these numbers is the only way to figure out how your websites are actually performing. And by keeping a record of these stats, it'll be easier for you to improve your website presence more and more.

So many times I've asked a host, 'By the way, do you like your website?'

And their lack-lustre response has been, 'I don't know if it works?'

Then, when I've said to these hosts, 'But how many people visit your website, and how many convert from lookers into bookers?'

I end up being met with these sad words:

'I don't know how to check.'

Now, the good news is that there are plenty of free tools which will help you with this. You don't need to go spending big money or go get a degree in digital marketing or computer science.

When plugged into your website (and this is why a Wordpress website is key here, because it gives you the ability to plug in these tools, while other CMS options are limited) you can grab access to all the information you need, so that you understand your website's performance inside-out.

Though I'd recommend reading about the brilliance of a Wordpress website in Chapter One, if you haven't already. This will help you at this stage of your business set-up, even more.

To help you even further, I've taken the liberty of updating the 'tools' in the resources section on the bookdirectplaybook.com (that virtual companion course that I keep referring to).

These useful website-related numbers that we've been referring to in this part of the Playbook are known as 'website analytics'. The beauty of geeking out on your analytics is that they'll give you the power to make the right changes to your online platforms if need be, and monitor their performance along the way. This is pure gold when it comes to marketing activity as well, which is the topic we're going to move onto next!

I'm very excited about diving into the marketing content, squad. This is my domain and perhaps the aspect of business I love most!

But before I get too carried away in my excitement, let me set you your next mini GID Session. It's simply to access the bookdirectplaybook. com and go and grab the tools you need (for website analytics). Be sure to implement them ASAP. Without knowing your analytics, you're likely shooting towards a goal with your eyes closed (and that rarely ends in success).

THE HIGHLIGHTS

I've spent the first part of this Playbook getting your land in order.

We've moved that 'house' of yours, which was built on sinking sand, onto solid concrete.

In other words, we've covered structures and systems, and reiterated the importance of a customer avatar.

There's a reason why I've repeated the term 'Customer Avator' more than any other phrase so far in this Playbook. To put it simply, a failure to understand this will result in a failure of scaling your hospitality business. Without it, you can't possibly build a successful website or blog - as we've also just covered.

Your guests are the most important part of your business, please spend time getting to know them (properly).

So, that's your biggest takeaway so far.

Know your guests, and then know how to implement that knowledge into your STR business.

Next up, we move onto marketing. Now, this is truly my area of expertise, so I'm going to show you some of my best moves.

Ensure that you've absorbed all the content in this Playbook so far, so we can confidently move onto the stuff that is going to take your hospitality business to phenomenal heights.

As we like to say at Boostly, **buckle up** - you're in for a soaring ride.

HALF
TIME

WHAT ARE YOUR MAIN TAKE AWAYS SO FAR?

Send me a DM on Instagram

 @boostlyuk

Enjoying the book so far?

Leave a review on
Amazon and send proof to
info@boostly.co.uk
for a special (bonus) training!

SECOND
HALF

Yes. I know. I have claimed this in nearly every chapter of the Playbook, but what's about to come really is one of the key aspects of your hospitality business.

In fact, I would go as far as saying that the following content is key for **any business.** You can quote me on that; and while you're at it, check out the quote below:

IT'S NOT WHAT YOU KNOW IT'S WHO YOU KNOW

I was wisely advised during the very early stages of my Boostly journey, that **'Your Network is Your Net Worth'.**

I shrugged it off at first, thinking I was being fed yet another regurgitated business quote. But the further into my business journey I went, the more those words began to ring true. Every business achievement and career boost has 100% been a result of the relationships (or partnerships) that I've closely nurtured.

And you know, this is the bit where I realise how bloody grateful we should be as business owners. Because it's never really just down to 'us'. It's a team effort. Just like soccer.

My personal journey would have been a lot harder, a lot trickier, and with far more obstacles, had I not had people in my tribe spreading the word about me and being valued advocates of my services and products.

In the same way, you need to become the go-to person in your area for short-stay accommodation. This will pay back tenfold, and is probably the most rewarding way of winning new business.

And the most exciting part about this chapter is that a lot of you reading this will already have many phone numbers, friendships, and names you can reach out to that could very easily result in 5 to 6 figure bumps in your revenue for the next 12 months.

You probably just haven't leveraged it in the way that you could (and should). I should give you a heads up, a lot of the stuff that we're about to cover in the following pages might take you out of your comfort zone.

THE
BOOK DIRECT
PLAYBOOK

IT'S NOT WHAT YOU KNOW, IT'S WHO YOU KNOW

'He only got that job because of his connections' was a throw-away remark by an old work colleague of mine back in London.

He was venting his frustration to me in a pub after a day in our stuffy office, in the middle of Oxford Circus. You know the drill.

The person my colleague was talking about had just got a manager's position in the sales room we all worked in.

'He only got it because he knows the hiring manager,' he repeated, as he angrily sipped on his pint of cider.

'And?' was my genuine reply.

I wasn't bitter, nor the slightest bit sour, unlike my friend, who was in full-blown rant mode by this point.

What my dear friend wouldn't say, nor wanted to admit, was that he was very much his own person, in his own world. He would turn up to work, shut himself off, and just work.

Now, there's nothing wrong with 'doing the work', but this lad was doing it all alone. When someone would ask for help or if they needed something, he would quite bluntly turn them away.

But the person who'd bagged the promotion was actively helpful, friendly, and made a real effort to build relationships in the office. So, when it came to the question of who should become a manager, the answer was too easy.

It wasn't even that this new manager was the smartest employee in the office. Nor the coolest. Nor the best dressed. Nor did he even smash sales goals every month.

He simply became the **'go-to'**...

He had demonstrated a quality that my friend, who was as bitter as the lemon in his cider, was never able to. He demonstrated the art of **building relationships**. And that remained top-of-mind.

So, let's get back to you, squad. What can you take from this story?

Are you like my friend who treats everyone as competition and keeps yourself to yourself in your local area? Or are you the person who is actively looking to build relationships and network in your area and become the go-to person when people are looking for accommodation?

More importantly, which would you prefer to be? **Which do you need to be?**

Hopefully you'll agree with me and choose option two. You might even be well on your way there.

But, if you're not - and you're secretly slipping into the bad habits of my old friend - then never fear. We're going to fix this for you.

The first thing I'd urge you to do is write the below quote on your wall, your fridge, your bathroom mirror...or just somewhere where you'll see it every day. No pressure:

> # IT'S NOT WHAT YOU KNOW, IT'S WHO YOU KNOW

You'll need to remember these glorious words as you're working through this chapter. They're absolute gold.

Also, keep repeating the following thought to yourself like a mantra: *It's not what they can do for you, it's what YOU can do for THEM.*

I appreciate that this might sound counterproductive right now, as I'm here to help **you** and your hospitality business. But let's focus on another easy tactic to help you understand my philosophy better.

This tactic takes no more than 15 minutes a day and will have you well on your way to becoming the ultimate 'Go-To'.

Hey, you'll probably be signing fan mail in no time.

BECOMING THE GO-TO GUY/GAL

For those who don't have an existing network, guests, or contacts you can call upon to start spreading the word of your business, this section is especially for you.

This tried and tested formula that I call '**becoming the go to**' works for any industry professional and any business owner.

It only takes a small amount of time a day to do but the secret is to stay consistent with it.

In other words, you need to show up every day.

But remember, only for 15 magic minutes. That's all you need.

I will do my best to explain the whole process in the book, however if you want an over the shoulder view of how to do this, then head to bookdirectplaybook.com for a tutorial video.

First up, find 3-5 online forums, obviously relating to what it is that you do business-wise.

For this example, and to make life easy, I am going to talk about Facebook Groups. However, please feel free to duplicate this for any channel or website forum out there.

What you're going to do is go to the Facebook Dashboard.

Head to the search function, where you'll run a few searches.

You're specifically looking for a maximum of 5 groups.

And here, we're going to adopt the 60/30/10 split, which I will also cover in the Hashtags section in the **Social Media Chapter**.

60% is going to be your niche
30% is going to be your location
10% is going to be a broad search

Now, on your phone or computer, find the groups around your niche/location/broader search. Then, save the links to these groups in your notes.

Next, go into the group and filter the searches to **recent posts** - not activity, we're only looking for posts here.

Once this is all done, then all you need to do every day is spend no more than 15 minutes going into the 3-5 groups and 'give value'. Value can be the form of anything. In your case, it'll mostly be answering questions.

Facebook Groups are built for people who need help. If you're looking for people you can offer value (and solutions) to, then Facebook Groups are a magnet for it. People these days, especially within our industry, are more likely to ask a question in a Facebook Group rather than on Google, because they appreciate the 'human' input, based on actual real-life experiences and learnings.

I adopted this simple tactic not only for The Grainary, but Boostly as well, and it worked a treat.

It can seem futile when you're doing it every day; but if you do it over a stretched period of time then the rewards, my friends, are massive. This, once again, is a great lesson in consistency and how doing little things over and over again can get you the results you want. It's not rocket science, and thinking that it is, is the first mistake hosts make.

Not only will you achieve monetary results eventually, but the above will help you get recognised as an authority in your field and really help build your rep. Which, needless to say, is fantastic for business.

Now, what's also key here is to make sure your personal profile on Facebook is also optimised so when someone comes to check out your profile, it is clear what you do, who you help, and how people can get in touch.

- Make sure your bio is up to date and there's a link to your website.

- Make sure your business page is linked to your personal profile, so people can view it.

You don't get the stats from Facebook on this, but you will be amazed at how many people will view your personal Facebook profile from a group.

Trust me, the results of being present, providing value, and helping people without asking for anything in return, are well worth it. Often, the hardest part for business owners (let alone hosts) to understand is to NOT directly sell themselves nor their business. This takes the very essence out of what you're trying to achieve, and while it may seem like a 'quick win', hard sells won't serve you as well, long term.

So, focus on the trust and relationship building first.

For example, where Boostly is concerned, if you were to visit any Facebook group now (hospitality related) and spot a post from a host asking for recommendations for a website designer, I can guarantee you that Boostly will get mentioned at least once.

This is because I have religiously implemented my aforementioned tactics for at least 12 months. Not once did I ask for anything in return (nor expected it), I simply helped and answered questions.

THE
BOOK DIRECT
PLAYBOOK

WORKING WITH LOCAL BUSINESSES

There's s a heap of benefits in building local connections and partnerships within your area with other businesses.

Once again, the specific benefits here are two-fold.

You can recommend said businesses to your guests. And, said businesses can recommend you to their customers.

We've generated countless bookings through building connections and partnerships with local operators. And it's not just hospitality operators either.

One of the best things I did after joining The Grainary was getting involved with the local BNI (Business Networking International). You will have one near you, as it's a worldwide organisation. You know, the one where they meet up once a week (normally over breakfast) and have a conversation about what's been happening in the business world over the past few days.

Now, I know there's a bit of a 'stigma' attached to these meet-ups, with many claiming that they're overly salesy and all-in-all a waste of time. However, approaching anything with that kind of mindset is never going to do you any favours.

Instead, go in with an open mind and you might discover that BNI is a fantastic accountability group and provides great networking opportunities.

They also have a 'no competitor clause'. So, if you're lucky enough to have no other hospitality business in the BNI group, then you can go in and quickly become the 'go to accommodation provider' within that area.

Also, the people attending these meetings may well become your best customers or brand ambassadors, if you play your cards right.

This is so easy to do with the right mindset, approach, and attitude - especially when you consider that in the corporate world, everybody knows everybody else. They're all part of the same circle and they want to refer businesses to their contacts, because it positions them as an authority too.

Another thing to remember about corporates is that they know of many professionals who are likely travelling in and out of the area for meetings and business opportunities. In this case, very few of them will have a recommended 'partner programme' for accommodation and will simply fall back on the option of an OTA or a well-known hotel chain.

This is where you can get your name in and become the go to. It's a huge gap in the market for you.

Normally at these BNI meetings, you'll have at least 10 other businesses in attendance. Consider, everyone attending is looking to boost their reputation and help other members succeed (they know this will be great for their business, too). So, if you're struggling to find a network where you can work on becoming the 'go to' then this is an excellent place to start.

Another great idea is to write a list of the local businesses and companies where you enjoy spending your money. This could be your favourite takeaway, bar, or events supplier. Then, give them a call and offer to recommend their services to your guests; there's almost a 100% chance that they'll warm to the idea straight away.

I don't know of anyone who's turned me down, after I've said:

'Would you like to make more money?'

You can even negotiate an exclusive discount for your guests and maybe a referral programme where you will get a kickback for each person you pass their way (more on that in the next section).

From there, it's up to you how you present the recommendation to your guests - and don't be afraid to be as creative as you like here.

Finally, look to build a local network of other accommodation providers who you can work with to pass bookings onto. You can do this via a private WhatsApp group, Facebook group, or even an email list.

How many times do you get a phone call or email from a Future Potential Guest, but you can't accommodate them? It's bound to have happened to you at some point.

So, instead of saying, 'sorry no', collect their information, dates, and budget and say:

'I can help. I will be in touch.'

Then go to your network and ask who can accommodate.

A lot of the time, you'll be able to create a WIN WIN WIN!

Win for the host who you're going to pass the booking to.

Win for the guest, as they have a place to stay.

Win for you, as you can work out a referral fee with the host so you can make money by simply passing on the booking.

Let's dive more into that now.

THE
BOOK DIRECT
PLAYBOOK

REFERRAL SCHEMES AND KICKBACKS

Always Dangle The Carrot

One of the quickest and fastest ways to grow your business is to build a referral programme.

I have tried and tested this with both my family business and Boostly. And yes, I have witnessed it work firsthand, not just for myself but for some of the biggest businesses in the world.

The problem is that here in the UK, I've noticed that the majority of British professionals don't like the sound of the word 'affiliates.' They think it's scammy.

My American friends, on the other hand, seem more open to the idea.

Referrals, kickbacks, affiliates, whatever you want to call it, this is my take on the whole concept:

'The more I grow my business directly off-the-back of someone recommending me, the more I want to give back and say thank you.' (And this works both ways).

At this point, I really ought to mention that none of the above has to be associated with money nor 'fiscal gains'. For example, I have sent gift hampers, vouchers, and days out in the past as a thank you to hosts who have recommended Boostly. Sometimes, people prefer these gestures even more.

But the one main thing that I've learnt is that people, when asked to do something (i.e. leave a review), need to have some form of incentive to do so. Not because they're not giving people, but we all need that extra nudge from time to time.

I'm going to deep dive into Social Media Giveaways in the next chapter, but just to quickly touch upon it now. Imagine sharing a post on social media and asking people to simply 'Like' the post as a favour to you. Unfortunately, very few people will engage because there is nothing on offer to excite them.

However, adding something as simple as, 'Like this post and you could win a prize' could see the number of likes on that very post skyrocketing. It's partly to with that innate competitive edge that's built into human beings; and also because of the simple fact that we all love freebies (even if it's a pen and you already have hundreds of pens stacked in your bedside drawer).

But going back to reviews, one of the reasons we were able to rank as the Top 3 on Tripadvisor in our county at one point, was that we made a real active effort to collect them in the first place. We actually asked for reviews on TripAdvisor, after providing stellar service, of course.

However, when asking our valued guests for these reviews, we would promise to enter them into a quarterly prize draw, where the winner would receive a free two-night stay with us in the future. Suddenly, there was a great incentive for people to spare a few minutes of their time to leave a review for our business.

The best part is, we found on a number of occasions that more than one person from each booking party would leave a review, to maximise their chances of winning the prize.

It was easy money in our pockets. The cost of offering two free nights for our business was far lower than all the extra bookings we generated because of these very reviews (and it was an opportunity for our guests to engage with us more, too!).

People love to win.

At Boostly, after a few years I added in an affiliate program properly and installed software that would actively track when current customers promoted Boostly to others that I wouldn't always hear about.

This has truly stepped up the business's performance.

Now, I get an email in my inbox when someone purchases a service from Boostly off the back of a recommendation. So I know exactly who's responsible for that extra business, for me. That person then automatically receives 10% of those service fees as a gesture of good will.

Not only is this smart business, but there's a real 'feel good' vibe about it too. Knowing that a friend, colleague, or contact of mine is able to treat themselves with that little extra cash in their pockets, simply for mentioning Boostly to a potential customer, it genuinely brings a smile to my face and reminds me of why I love what I do.

Over the years, I've extended this tactic (beyond direct customers and clients) and have struck partnerships with other businesses within the hospitality industry.

And you can, too.

Imagine how powerful it would be to build a network in your area where you're all 'passing the bookings'. And not only this, but you're all earning a referral fee in the process.

And before you say 'well that's not a direct booking...'

It is!

Remember, a direct booking is not always about the money you take. The most important commodity in the world is data. It's what the big companies in the world are striving for.

So, when you get a guest book directly with you, the most important thing to remember is that it is on your terms. It's your rules; and you're never at the mercy of somebody else's say-so.

Ultimately, if you give 5% of a booking to another host for getting you a booking, then so be it. You're still winning (spectacularly) in the process. And the value is massive because you've kept the booking in your community.

Could you create a text message group of local hosts and when someone calls or enquires and you can't take the booking, instead of saying:

'No, sorry,' and hanging up...

You get their details and say that you will be in touch in a few hours.

Jump in your text messaging group and get them placed. Then you simply pass the booking on for the new host to contact, complete the booking, and you still get some form of revenue.

Depending on the booking, this could result in a 4 or 5 figure bump in your revenue over the course of 12 months.

Finally, which businesses that aren't in your industry could you build up referral programs with? Is there someone locally, for example a transport company? Could you build up a partnership where they will become your number one recommended company to your guests when they arrive and need transport to your company? When they book with them, you get a referral fee.

And vice versa, imagine the amount of people they get coming through their business everyday, and there's an active advertisement for your business.

What I want for you to do with this section is to think about how you can implement this into your business.

Look at how you're rewarding your current guests for recommending you.

How can you build a referral network in your local community?

Do you need software to do this or can you do it offline?

The best place to start, and this is what we're going to talk about next, is in your phone book right now.

'DO YOU KNOW ANYONE?'

There's a story I remember that I was told by a host based in the UK which sums up why I believe that building relationships in any business is the key to success.

Ryan Luke had just started to rent out accommodation he had acquired in his local area. Instead of getting tenants, he had decided to rent it out short stay.

The problem was he didn't know where to start.

One morning, after having a heavy night out and sporting a hangover, he decided to pick up the most important marketing tool in his arsenal: his mobile phone.

He loaded up his contacts and texted the same thing to anyone he met the previous night whilst in the pubs and clubs.

I paraphrase this text because as he was telling me this story, I was trying to frantically remember this, because it's genius.

I'll try my best:

> 'Hey buddy, you said last night that someone was coming to town and needed a place to stay, who was that again?'

He sent it en masse.

Texts came back:

> 'What you talking about Ry?'

> 'I didn't see you last night, did I!??'

Then, there was the golden nugget:

> 'Oh yeah, I remember, here's his number, give him a call.'

That text resulted in bookings for his property.

No social media algorithms

No SEO

No marketing

No cold calling

A simple text message.

'Do you know anyone' is so powerful.

But it's one that we don't use enough.

You don't have to go on a night out, you can start right now and maintain your sobriety (and health) while doing so.

One of the easiest things you can do right now is look at the guests who have stayed with you over the past year. You can get access to this via your bookings and reports. Then, give them a call.

You're basically going to ask if they know anyone who's going to be travelling to the area anytime soon.

For some of you, this may be hard to do (on any platform) and might make you feel slightly uncomfortable. However, this entire Playbook is about making you comfortable about being uncomfortable.

But, if you'd like a hand with this or even a template to get things moving, then simply head on over to my online companion course where I've got you covered:

Bookdirectplaybook.com

There's ideas for content/'scripts' in here that you can edit to your own liking and move forward with.

After you've spoken to your past guests, I recommend that you move onto the world of social media. Remember, all you have to do is ask.

I'm going to move on to social media in full in the next chapter, but for now all you're going to do is put the word out. This can be on your own personal feed, or in a forum you may be part of.

The text can be:

> I have accommodation in {INSERT AREA} which is available for people coming to stay.
>
> If you know anyone who needs a place to stay please get in touch.

If you want to add in at this point that you have a referral programme in place, that will help you dangle the metaphorical carrot.

Another great idea is to call your trusted contacts (anybody who knows, likes, and trusts you) and ask them the following question:

> 'Hey, do you know anyone who needs accommodation? I have a few rooms/units available.'

This should naturally be easier to do with your friends, which will in turn help ease your nerves when it comes to people you haven't yet built a personal relationship with.

Now, I'm not for a minute suggesting that you call your friends everyday with the same question; there's a fine line between excellent marketer and plain old annoying.

However, putting out the feelers now and again will definitely increase your chances of generating more direct bookings. So many people forget that the greatest tool we have in our arsenal is PEOPLE. There's no harm in asking the question now and again.

THE
BOOK DIRECT
PLAYBOOK

MORE CORPORATE BOOKINGS

To finish this chapter I wanted to share with you some actionable tactics and tips that you can implement into your business right now to help get more corporate bookings.

When it comes to corporate bookings, there's a big split in the world of hospitality as to the mindset towards this. They either have a strong income based on business bookings, or they don't, because they believe that their business wouldn't ever appeal.

A good friend of mine and amazing sales and business coach, Jessica Lorimer, has built a business by coaching business owners how to build corporate revenue into their business. I recommend you check out her podcast, 'Selling to Corporates' as it's one of the best resources for learning more about the corporate world.

One of the key stats she shared with me and my Boostly Academy members during an exclusive training course, was this:

The average B2C Transaction was £1.5k

The average B2B Transaction was a little over £10k

That's 5x the value!

And Jessica also dispelled the myth that corporate businesses are the 'Amazons' of the world by stating that in the dictionary, it states that a corporate company has a few members of staff.

Corporate bookings or business bookings are not hard to come by either.

I think that so many hospitality owners see it as an avenue so hard to get into, that they don't bother.

However, there's often a high chance that you already have a great network of potential business bookings, simply by going through the reports of your previous bookings.

So why not revisit all the bookings you've received over the last 12 months? Go through each one. See if you can spot any email addresses in there that look like they have a business domain. 99% of the time a leisure guest will book with you via their personal account; so you can quite easily rule them out.

Once you've collated a list of the right business email addresses (and if you can gather phone numbers, even better), then give these corporate guests a call. Remember, as they've already stayed with you they're more likely to like and trust you.

So, this doesn't have to be labelled as that dreaded 'cold call' that so many business people are afraid of. Reframe it in your mind: it's simply a friendly catch up call.

During this light-hearted conversation, try and figure out if the person you're speaking to visits your area regularly, or if they know anybody else who does.

Depending on who you're conversing with and how this catch up goes, this could go one of two ways. It could be the case where they are the one to directly speak to, or they will be able to put you in touch with the PA or accommodation officer at their company. If it's the latter, then it will require another phone call, but this could be the start of a fantastic business relationship.

The key to more business bookings, as Jessica will remind you, is to know your numbers.

If it helps, before you start calling, work out a price per head for corporate businesses. What you will find is that they have a budget per head for their staff that they need to get accommodation for.

Each company will be different for what they need and require for their staff, but the only way you're going to find out is by calling.

Because we're going to start by going in via a previous guest, the conversation is so much easier.

> 'Hi {NAME}, {GUEST'S NAME} recommended I give you a call. They recently stayed with us and we got to talking about his peers who travel to our area often. He mentioned that you have difficulty finding places to stay, so I said I would get in touch to introduce myself and see if we can help with housing members of your staff. He said that you're the best person to speak to, is this right?'

Depending on how that initial 30 seconds go, you're going to get a few answers.

Yes.

No.

Yes, but not right now.

The trick is to stay calm, remember you're speaking to a human, and to be polite. If you focus on those three things then good things will happen.

And if you mess up, stumble your words, and have an awful call, then don't worry, there's plenty more places to call and contact.

After exhausting the list of past guests, you can look at your local area. There are so many places to look that you probably hadn't even thought of before.

For example sports clubs. Professional or semi-professional clubs in your area are always needing accommodation.

Let me share with you another story of a conversation I was having with a host.

This host is an accidental hospitality owner. He had two houses which he owned in Scotland.

He wasn't based in any of the major cities, but a town on the outskirts of Glasgow.

His son was training for one of the lower league football teams in the country; for which the host would take him to down to every evening.

After one of the training sessions, he got speaking to the scouts at the club. They were chatting about what they were doing and the conversation soon focused on one of his homes.

It turned out that he had recently lost his long-term tenants and was looking to see what to do next. His initial idea was actually to sell the properties.

But the scout mentioned that there were a few agents coming to town and they were in need of accommodation because the usual hotel they use was fully booked due to a big demand in weddings.

It was late August and the football season was about to start and the club needed to sign a few players. This host said that his property was ready to accommodate guests straight away and was put in contact with the club's secretary.

What resulted off the back of this was a solid year's worth of bookings from not only that club, but others in the area.

And, of course, recommendations.

Not only did he not have to sell the properties, he actually expanded his portfolio and was also able to create another income stream, by getting bookings for when the clubs and other businesses needed a place to stay.

And before you assume that this was a big professional club in the premier division, it wasn't. This was lower league where the budget isn't in the millions.

Now, look at what is around you.

Are there sports clubs?

Are there places you wouldn't think of normally approaching?

Again, we assume that they have a recommended accommodation list. But many don't and when they need to find accommodation, they simply head to the big online travel agents.

Be proactive, put a call in and introduce yourself.

And the same goes with the event venues in your area. How many conferences or expos do you have in your area on an annual basis?

And again, we assume that all of these venues have accommodation lists that they place their delegates in. They don't.

Drop a call in and put your name down.

And after all of the above, if you still have no idea, go to your local council's website. That's another opportunity right there. You can look for the upcoming projects that have been given the green light. With their 'Freedom of Information Act', they HAVE to show you who has won the project.

With a big project, they will need accommodation. A quick search on the internet and you will be able to find the main contact details for the head office.

If you're smart and proactive, you will be able to phone the office and ask to find out who will be in charge of placing their staff or contractors for the upcoming project.

The worst that they will say is no.

So be proactive, and get calling.

There will be a lot of you reading this who will try and hide behind an email. Please don't.

In a world and age where we're all emailing, texting, and sending messages online, picking up the phone and having a conversation is a lost art.

As long as you remember the three rules:

Stay calm

Remember you're speaking to a human

Be polite

You will get more yes's than no's.

GET IT DONE

I have given you a lot of actionable tactics in this chapter.

What I want for you is to take one thing, put a plan down and take action.

I'm so confident that in this one chapter alone, you will get income coming into your business if you action it.

The key is to be proactive and START CONNECTING.

When you do, send me a message on Instagram @boostlyuk. I would love to see your results.

Recently, I was intrigued about what #TeamBoostly members associated me with most. I teach a lot of aspects of marketing for hosts about how to increase their bookings, but I wanted to find out how they 'viewed me'. What did they first think of when it comes to me and what I teach?

The answer was: social media.

I do love social media. I attribute not only the popularity of the family business to it, but also Boostly as well. It's a free tool that anyone can utilise to grow the awareness of your business.

The problem is that it's still relatively new, if you compare it to all the other marketing tactics out there. And because of that, people are still figuring out how to use it properly.

A large majority of businesses I see use it all wrong. They treat it like a magazine or a tv advert.

Sell

Sell

Sell

There's a big clue in the name:

SOCIAL media.

Think about it, the last time you loaded up Facebook on your phone or laptop, you weren't going on there to browse for something to buy. You went on to see what's happening in your world or network.

You wanted to see what your 'Facebook Friends' are doing, engage in a group or community you're part of, or to just scroll the feed.

It's the same with the other channels.

Each channel has its own power and tribe.

This chapter could easily be a deep dive into each individual channel where I would share with you tactics and tips for each one. The problem with that would be the training and tactics could, and most probably would, be out of date before the book is even printed.

Social Media Channels will come and go.

Some will get bigger, some will change names, and each channel and network will bring in new features and lose ones that don't work.

Instead, in this chapter I want to share with you tactics and tips that are evergreen and tap more into the psychology of people and how they use social media, so that you can replicate it on each channel.

I'm going to share with you my secret sauce in how I have used social media for the past 15 years to grow a massive network of people who happily recommend me to their friends and peers, and also the guide to how I create so much content and easily apply it to a busy day.

Social media is so powerful to growing your business and increasing your direct bookings.

By the end of this chapter I'm going to change your mindset on how to use it.

By the end of this chapter you will be like Neo in *The Matrix* when he realises the power that he truly holds.

I had my 'Matrix moment' in 2016 when I started to see social media differently and it totally transformed how I used it.

There will be some Get It Done Sessions, so make sure you keep an eye out for that. There will also be some sections where you will need to see what I'm talking about, so you will need to head over to the bookdirectplaybook.com

And, for full transparency, I do have a product that will help with your social media.

Boostlycontentcreator.com

It was created because hosts just like you asked for it.

I'm not going to actively mention it in this chapter, but I wanted to do it now so you know that if during this chapter you think you need help, I want to let you know I created something that will.

If you're not a member of the content creator movement, then please do check it out.

Every penny brought into the membership is reinvested back into the members to make it bigger, better, and stronger.

It started as an idea and now has over 1000 hosts around the world who never have to worry about what to post on their channels, what emails to send, and how to appeal to their ideal guest.

Let's begin.

THE
BOOK DIRECT
PLAYBOOK

SOCIAL MEDIA SECRET SAUCE

When I first joined the family business on a full time basis, my main task was to get the farm online.

We had just moved back to Scarborough after spending time in London where I worked for one of the biggest review websites in the world.

At that business, I was introduced to the power of social media. Facebook and Twitter were growing in power and influence into our day-to-day lives. With the introduction of the iPhone and other devices that made the internet more easily accessible, people everywhere were starting to spend more time on their mobile devices.

Instead of playing Snake on their phones, they were utilising social media.

I don't know where this ability has come from, but I seem to have developed a very good intuition on how and where the trends are going and where people's attention is at the right time.

I have also been very lucky to be able to follow and get to know some of the brightest marketing minds in the world, thanks to the masterminds and communities I joined.

When I moved back to the farm, I set out to get the Grainary online as soon as possible.

WHEN EVERYONE ZIGS, YOU ZAG

I looked at what other hospitality businesses were doing and I could see that they were not adapting to this new social world that was coming.

Social media is great for small businesses because you can get started for free. All you have to pay is **TIME.**

For full context and transparency, the Grainary was 20 years into its business journey when I joined and I was lucky to be able to tap into 20 years worth of guests and previous customers. However, what I am going to show you in this section can be replicated for businesses of any age or part of their startup journey.

I know that those who consume this book will be at different points in their journey; I'm fully aware of this. But this is something I did for 18 months for the family business and it helped us grow to become the biggest local independent business within the area. It was simple to do, and the best part? It didn't cost me a single penny.

The trick is this.

Post On Social Media Every Day.

That's it.

Now, before you shake your head in disgust, dear reader, hear me out.

Listen to any successful business owner, watch any YouTube interview with some of the most powerful business owners in the world, and they will share with you the same trait.

Consistency

Consistency is boring

It's not fancy

It's not a get rich quick scheme

But it has fantastic long lasting results.

Consistency is King

And social media is no different.

If you post on social media every day for the next 365 days, then good things will happen to you and your business.

Now, I know there will be some who will be thinking:

> 'Well, I have posted every day for the past year and nothing has come of it.'

Well, I say this with the biggest smile on my face:

What you have posted is crap.

Or, what you have posted has been more sales than social. You have turned off your audience and followers. You have likely bored the life out of them if all you've been doing is 'selling stuff'. Or, even worse, you have wasted your time speaking to the wrong people.

Now, honestly, look back at what you have posted and tell me in a direct message on Instagram @boostlyuk if I'm wrong.

I will be more than happy to quickly look over your posts and let you know. And I'll be bluntly honest with you, too (for your own good).

I've executed thousands of mini marketing reviews over the years and time and time again, the reason why hosts are not getting any traction or getting tumbleweed on social media is because they are using social media to primarily sell.

Let's go back to what I said at the start of this chapter:

People do not open up their social media to buy.

It is not Amazon.

So stop using it like that.

One of the first things that every hospitality business needs to do is go to their business page or channel and change their profile picture.

So many people hide behind their logo or brand.

Again, this is NOT the shopping channel.

It is your Social Media Channel.

People want to see the face behind the business. Human beings are social creatures who are far more likely to warm to the whites of your eyes than the white background on a corporate logo.

So please, change the profile picture to a photo of you, or you and your team.

For bonus points, it's better to keep that profile photo the same throughout all your social media platforms. You can check out how I've done this for Boostly on my socials. It's the same throughout - a picture of my instantly recognisable face against a bright background.

I appreciate that for some of you this might seem a bit daunting, or perhaps you're worried that you don't have many interesting things to say, in a world outside of boring sales posts?

But never fear, the rest of this chapter will give you loads of content ideas - content inspiration - that you can use for your business right away.

And if you're consistent and stick to the tactics that I'm about to share with you for the next 365 days, then the results will come - I promise.

And if they don't, then you have permission to message or email me on day 365 and I will refund you the full amount you paid for this book.

You have my word.

THE SIMPLE GUIDE TO CONTENT CREATION

'I know I need to do more, but I don't know where to start.'

I was speaking to a member of the hospitality community on a coaching call.

She was having a mental block.

It's the same for so many other people I speak to.

This member had a Facebook page. The problem was that the posts were few and far between, and when she did post, it was simply a share from another business page.

It resulted with a social media presence that had less life than a ghost town.

'Does social media actually work?' was her next comeback.

'Yes,' I said.

'Especially when you do it right,' I continued.

What I'm going to share with you in this section is exactly what I told her and hundreds of other people who were tuning in to that coaching call live.

This brave owner had put her hand up to be featured on a live coaching call with me on Facebook and to be part of the Boostly Podcast.

Her name was Nicola, and I should mention that I actually checked her Facebook page before writing this section of the book and I was mighty proud to see the improvements. (Go, Nicola!)

The best part of Nicola's efforts was that she actually enjoyed it; so much so that it naturally became a part of her day-to-day business routine. The business now has a visible presence online and her followers engage far more as they feel a part of her exciting journey.

All because of content creation.

These two words are hard to get your head around when you're first starting out.

'What do I post?'

'What would people like to see?'

I get it.

This is where it's important that before you start to research or create content, you have to know your customer avatar. It is one of the first chapters in this book. If you haven't gone through that chapter first, I recommend you head back to it and master that section before coming back here. Once you know who you're creating content for, this becomes a whole lot easier.

I'm going to continue to write this section and chapter with the view that you know your customer avatar, what they like, dislike, want to know.

The best way to answer the question:

'What would people like to see?' is simply following these steps.

I'm going to share with you a few websites I currently use. This list will be updated on the companion course at bookdirectplaybook.com as I'm aware that over time some of the sites may change or cease to exist. However, at the time of writing this book, the following websites will still help you in bucket loads. Take your time in getting to know them.

ANSWERTHEPUBLIC.COM

This website is unknown by so many people, but it is a fantastic tool for trying to figure out what your customer avatar is searching for online.

You get to have a certain amount of searches for free before you need to upgrade, but you can get everything you need from the free account.

I will show you how to use the website on bookdirectplaybook.com but in simple terms, this website will be able to give you a list of questions that people are asking for in your niche or location.

What I recommend you do is find 1-3 questions, write them down on a piece of paper, and move on to the next resource.

QUORA.COM

Similar to Answerthepublic, Quora is a free question and answer based website.

Unfortunately, because of scummy marketers, the questions now have become segways into said marketers answering their own questions promoting their services.

This is the problem with amazing tools and ideas like Quora. Marketers are always there to try and beat the system.

Now, this doesn't mean that it isn't a good resource. You can still search for questions that your avatar is looking for online.

You might need to set up a 'scummy marketer filter' in your mindset before you use it.

Unlike Answerthepublic.com this is a 100% free tool.

Again, I have created a video on bookdirectplaybook.com showing you how to use this website.

FACEBOOK GROUPS

If you're looking for the most up to date and real time resources on how to find what your customer avatar is asking right now, then Facebook Groups are the best tool to use.

For a start, they are free and you don't have to pay any money to get the answers. And the beauty is once you have set up this system, it will take no time at all to find out what your ideal guest is searching and asking online.

Here's what you need to do:

1 | Create a note, document or sheet on your computer

2 | Create columns
Facebook Group Name
Facebook Group URL
Group Size (How many members)
Admin Name
Admin Facebook Profile URL
Moderator's Name
Moderator's Facebook Profile URL

3 | Join the group and then rearrange the posts to 'recent posts' instead of 'recent activity'

4 | Save the URL as a favourite in your bookmarks as well as adding to the document you created.

Let's dig into a few of the actions above to explain.

The reason why you're going to make a note of the admin and the moderators is because they will potentially be your best new friends on Facebook in the future. The sooner you start building a relationship with the people who run the groups you're going to be part of, the better.

What's important to note at this stage is that you're going to look to join the Facebook Groups that are around your location and niche.

I would recommend you join 10 max.

Anymore than 10 and the admin becomes too much.

What you're looking to do is split it in a 60/30/10 ratio.

60% of the 10 you join will be in your niche.

For example, if your avatar is families, find groups on Facebook that are family vacation based.

30% of the 10 is going to be around your location.

Note: You can do your exact location and any county/state related groups.

And 10% is going to be peers in your industry.

This could be hospitality related groups, or other owners who run a business like yours.

This exercise takes 30 minutes to do, but will be valuable not only for this but also for another tactic I'm going to explain later in the book.

Before you ask, yes, I have recorded a video on how to do this at bookdirectplaybook.com

The next step is to access the groups that you have added to your list and filter to the latest posts. You're specifically looking for the questions that your customer avatar is asking. Get a really good idea of what's creating that itch in their brain.

This part could take 30-45 minutes to do because you're going to have to scroll through a number of irrelevant posts.

All you're looking for is 3 questions that get asked regularly and again write them down on the same piece of paper of questions you took from Answerthepublic and Quora.

By now, if you have done the first 3 steps correctly, you should have at least 9 common questions that your customer avatar is asking online.

And just like that, you have a collection of future content ideas that you can use for future posts.

FREQUENTLY ASKED QUESTIONS FROM YOUR GUESTS

Where better to find content to create based on the questions your customer avatar is asking than from your actual guests?

Now, I will caveat this by saying if you're a host who is just getting started and you're yet to have any guests, then this is not for you. However, you already have at least 9 questions to get started on, so you can afford to skip this and move on.

If you're fortunate to already have had guests stay with you, then your task is simple.

Go to your email inbox, your OTA inbox and your social media inbox.

Go through all of the questions your guests ask.

What you're looking for here is the 20% of questions that get asked 80% of the time.

Without me even looking, I instantly know what ours were for the family business.

Again, write these down on the same piece of paper.

From this simple task, you should now have at least 12 pieces of content to create.

Even if you just do one a month, you now have a year's worth of content.

The next step now is 'How do I create the content?' And if there's one thing I'm very good at, it is content creation. I'm about to lay out my secret sauce for you in the rest of this chapter.

So, be ready to become a content creating machine by the end of this.

SUCCESS LEAVES CLUES

B efore you head off and go and create the content around your questions, there's one more quick step you can do to see what is working online and in your niche.

Remember the 10% of groups that I asked you to join and add to your sheet in the previous section? Well, we did this to find other businesses in your niche that you can engage and build a relationship with (more on this later in the book).

What you're looking for here is 3-5 businesses that are doing social media well. It may take a while, but the beauty of Facebook is that you can find out everything about everyone on there.

You can start with the admins and the moderators of the group, and then filter to the most popular posts from the past 12 months. Find the people who are engaging and using the group well, and then click on their personal profile and they will have on there, their business page.

Find their business page and follow it. Make a note of the URL as well. Add it to a note or the same sheet/doc so you can save it for later.

Once you have your 3-5 business pages, head to your own business page and in the 'insights' section of your business page, you can go to pages and you can add other business pages in your niche that you can follow. Go and get the page names that you have already collected and add them in here.

Now, what you can do is filter the businesses and all of their posts and see which ones have received the most engagement.

Again, I have clearly shown this in a video on the bookdirectplaybook. com.

What you're looking for here is which type of content (video, written, audio) is getting the most engagement.

Make a note on which type of content works best and get inspiration to replicate it for your own content.

CREATE THE CONTENT

You now will be armed with what you're going to talk about and also which types of content work best for your type of business. A selection might be:

- Video
- Live Video
- Images
- Funny images/memes
- Storytelling posts
- Questions
- Audio

I strongly recommend for you not to overthink this, just do it.

This is why I love live videos. There's no stop and restart, you just learn to do. And even if you mess up, it's part of the fun. The followers will love to see that you're not perfect and you're trying something new.

Showcasing you and your personality is what social media is all about warts and all.

DONE IS BETTER THAN PERFECT

Remember, test, test, and test some more.

Don't worry about getting anything 'bang on' the first time. Your audience's reaction will guide you here, and they'll tell you what they want (and don't want) to see from you.

GET IT DONE

With all you have learnt in this chapter, this is where you get to stop and do.

The task for you is to create one piece of content based on what you have learnt above.

Upload it to your social media channel of choice and tag in @boostlyuk so I can see it.

REPURPOSING CONTENT

Repurposing content is one of the most important skills I have learnt in the past decade.

Learning this is a massive time saver tool and can help grow your channels.

What's more, if you have followed the outsourcing section of the book, then your life will be easier because you can find someone to do all of this for you.

I was explaining this to a host on a coaching call.

His response was:

'But Mark, I am running a hospitality business, why do I need to repurpose content like some fancy agency?'

My response was:

> 'Imagine starting from one piece of content that takes 30 minutes to create, and with that you could create enough additional posts that will get a lot of engagement and fill your calendar without worrying about creating anything else for 30 days?'

Imagine this.

You go live on Facebook and answer a question that is common from the searches you have done.

It takes 30 minutes.

From there, you pass the video to a virtual assistant who transcribes the live video and creates a blog post on your website.

The same VA also creates an image and uploads to your other social media channels.

Finally, the same VA takes the 30 minute video and chops it up to several smaller videos and uploads them to your channels and stories.

And all you have done is pick up your phone and talk for 30 minutes.

Everything else is created and uploaded whilst you're focusing on other aspects of your business.

That's the power of repurposing content.

WHICH SOCIAL MEDIA CHANNEL SHOULD I USE?

It's probably one of the most common questions I see in the forums and Facebook Groups. Which social media channel should I focus on?

Or worse, I have seen people asking, should I be on there (insert social media channel)?

The beauty of applying the previous section into your business is that you can be everywhere. Repurposing content is easy if you outsource it and it means you can be everywhere.

For example, with Boostly I record one video and then the people I outsource to repurpose it and chop it up and share it around all of the platforms. Then, all I do, once a day, is spend 5-25 minutes checking in on comments in direct messages on the platforms.

One of the key things I have learnt is never miss a virtual high five. If you get someone take the time out of their day to comment or send you a message with something positive, then I make sure I return the favour with a virtual high five back.

It can be as simple as a quick emoji, or a thank you, or maybe go the extra mile and send a quick voice note back. Everyone can afford a minute in their busy work day to respond.

The trick to this is to not try and multi-task.

When you are going to reply, block off 5-25 minutes in your calendar to focus on this. Trust me, if you try to multi-task and do it whilst doing something else, you will fail at this task.

The main thing to do here is to make sure you don't fall into the rabbit hole of scrolling through other people's posts and waste an hour when you could spend it being productive and interacting with your followers or peers who have got in touch.

There are productivity tools that you can install that will help with this so you don't get distracted. I have a updated list of resources available on bookdirectplaybook.com

So, when I get asked the question: 'Which social media channel should I be on?'

My simple answer is 'all of them.'

You'll soon realise that you can be present everywhere without giving up all your valuable time.

HASHTAGS & VISIBILITY

I alluded to this topic earlier in the Playbook (in the Customer Avatar Chapter). Now it's time to tell you more about it.

Did you know that there's a sure fire way to get your social media post to be seen by your customer avatar, which in turn increases the chances of you getting more direct bookings and boosting your revenue?

And best of all, you don't have to spend a penny on advertising!

Well it comes in the shape of 4 lines:

A hashtag, otherwise known as #.

A hashtag is a conversation starter.

A hashtag opens the gateway to you discovering your ideal guests.

A hashtag gives your post more reach and visibility.

I'm going to cover two main ways to use hashtags.

When you post on your social media channel next, remember that hashtags are a very powerful tool in your arsenal to get it seen.

This is called the Hashtag Formula.

Depending on who you're talking to, they have a variation of this.

This is my take.

Different channels allow different amounts of hashtags per post. The rule of thumb you should be using to get a post seen is the 60/30/10 rule:

60% of your hashtags need to be uber focused around your niche.

30% of your hashtags needs to be generic but still around your niche.

10% of your hashtags need to be uber generic.

Let's look at the focused ones first. These are specifically around your niche and will have very few other people talking about it online.

For this example, I've used the following, based on where my property is located (Scarborough) and that my customer avatar is a family looking for a farm stay vacation.

The uber focused hashtags could be: #familyfriendlyfarmstay #stayonafarmuk #farmie

The generic hashtags, but still slightly around the niche, would be: #Farmstay #bookdirect

And then the uber generic would be: #UkHolidays #Scarborough

I would then use those hashtags in my post.

By using this formula, you are giving yourself a massive chance to be seen for the hashtags used.

Instead of using 100% of your post to go for the generic hashtags that have thousands of views but are very hard to rank for, you're niching down slightly to give yourself more chance to be seen. See, hashtags aren't just things 'millenials' use, they're a great way of helping you get in front of more eyeballs.

Repeat the above process for each one of your posts, but try and mix the hashtags up a little (and keep track of the ones you think work best).

DISCOVERABILITY

If you were to open up your social media channel of choice right now, there would be a search function.

If you head to the search and tap in a hashtag around your niche, there is sure to be at least one person in the world who has posted or engaged in that hashtag.

For example, let's go and look at #bookdirect

You can type that in on any social media channel and what you're more than likely to see is other hosts from around the world who are using that hashtag to encourage their Future Potential Guests to book direct.

They will have created some form of content to discuss this further.

Or, this hashtag might be used by content creators or guests who have posted content and used that hashtag because they are working with the property itself, in one way or another.

Whatever the background story may be, a conversation has been started because of the hashtag and you can join in.

You can create a piece of content on your channel and when you do include the #bookdirect, your post will be added to the other people talking about it. It's a bit like being back in a school playground and talking about the same music groups that you've seen the popular kids in school getting exciting about. In both scenarios, you're looking to create a common ground, so that you're more likely to get heard.

What I recommend you do is think about what we chatted about in the Customer Avatar Chapter and think about what your Future Potential Guest might be chatting about online.

Think about which hashtags they might be following and engaging in.

Come up with 5 hashtags.

Then, write them down.

I normally spend 5-10 minutes doing this exercise.

The goal is to find new people to follow or engage with.

I will run the search of the hashtag for my ideal guest or peer I want to engage with and search for, and then I will look at the most recent content that has been created around it.

As discovered in the previous chapter, it's not what you know, it's who you know, and relationships and partnerships are one of the most attributed factors to a successful business.

So, as well as looking for your Future Potential Guest when you're searching on social media and via hashtags, also be looking to utilise hashtags where your peers are in the industry and around your niche.

Whatever you decide to go for, keep a note of which you use and look to engage for 5-10 minutes a day.

There are channels that are easier to do this on than others, but what I do is find accounts or posts that I like the look of and then I engage.

There is zero point doing this exercise if you're simply going to consume. You need to engage to get the attention of the person posting the content. A simple comment is the easiest way to do this. It doesn't have to be an essay, it can be a few words or perhaps ask a question.

If you do this enough over an allotted time, then they will start to recognise you, your profile picture, your name, and then they'll go and dig in and see what you do.

It's simple social media activity:

Person discovers your account.
They click in to find out more.

And then, if they like the look of your channel, they will delve further, maybe into your website or other channels.

And don't do what so many people do and jump from one account to the other.

Simply liking a few posts and then ghosting the individual.

When you do the daily check-in I would be spending 5-15 minutes doing this consistently.

Spend 5-15 minutes checking for when people engage with you.

And then 5-15 minutes discovering and engaging with other content.

Max 30 minutes a day over the course of 365 days.

Combine that with everything else I have shown you in this chapter and I guarantee you that good things will happen to you and your business.

The opportunities, conversations, and revenue that happens on the back end will be game changing to your profits.

GET IT DONE

What I want for you to do is open a notepad or create a sheet on your computer.

You're going to discover the main hashtags for your niche and location.

In one column you're going to write down 50 hashtags based on the tactics I covered in this section.

Then, you're going to label which channel each one is the most useful for you, for each hashtag.

This will become your Hashtag Playbook.

You can share this sheet with your team who are repurposing your content for you so they know which hashtags to aim for each time they post.

Also, once you have this list, you will be able to use it each day to discover new Future Potential Guests and also potential peers to partner and build a relationship with.

GIVEAWAYS

I would be remiss to create a chapter on social media and not mention giveaways.

With all the training I do, I believe this is the one where it gets the most results in the shortest time possible.

I attribute this one main tactic I implemented for The Grainary as to why we grew such a huge social media following in the shortest time frame.

Social media giveaways work because people love to win stuff.

It doesn't matter if you're giving away a holiday or a pen:

People love to win.

It's in our nature.

It's so powerful, and I am going to cover this...but not in this book.

I could probably write a whole book on this section alone, however I am also aware that I could give you some actionable tips and advice that you could do right now, but by the time it comes to print some of those tactics and training will be out of date.

What I have done instead is dedicate a whole training section to this on the free companion course that you get at bookdirectplaybook.com

This way, I can keep all of the videos and training updated as the rules, regulations, and social media channels update as we go.

Simply head to bookdirectplaybook.com watch the videos and implement.

Sometimes throughout the year I host a live 5 day training where we come together as a group of hosts and run a giveaway together at the same time.

I love these weeks because training when done as a group, where you have live accountability and a chance to work together, is so powerful.

We normally get 600 plus hosts from around the world joining in and the wins and results are amazing.

We have had some hosts who have brought in over £10k worth of new bookings in a space of one week directly on the back of this free training.

If this sounds like something you would like to be part of, simply head to boostly.co.uk/ical and I will make sure you get informed the next

time we run this.

I adore social media and am so excited to see what your takeaways are from this chapter and, more importantly, how you implement the changes into your business and the results you get off the back of it.

Before you move on to the next chapter, go and implement some of the tactics in here to your business and then send me a message on Instagram to tell me what you've done.

Even better, when you start to post and utilise the new hashtags into your strategy, tag in @boostlyuk and I will be able to see them in the wild and then engage with you.

The main thing to remember is to stop treating social media like Amazon.

Social always sells.

People buy from people.

You just need to showcase your personality.

EMAIL MARKETING

Just in case you've flipped to this section of the Playbook first, I want to remind you that this entire book is created with the goal to help you detach yourself from controlling OTAs and reclaim control.

NEVER BUILD YOUR HOUSE ON SOMEONE ELSE'S LAND

How do you ensure that?

Well, a key way of doing this is by being proactive (and smart) with your marketing.

What if I told you there was one marketing activity that you can do that costs no money? That is super effective. One where you can track exactly who engages with your content.

It was, is, and will always be, the best marketing activity out there.

Yes, you've guessed it. Email marketing. A topic that many know I speak very frequently about.

The best way to describe email marketing to you is this:

In marketing there are two lanes:

The Slow Lane

The Fast Lane

The end destination is to make a transaction with you, the business owner.

The Slow Lane is a customer who does the following:

- Visits your website

- Sees a social media post

- Checks out your listing on an OTA

- Views your Google Business map listing

- Hears about you from a friend or co-worker

The Fast Lane is getting them into your database and sending carefully crafted emails that will turn Lookers into Bookers.

Why is this?

Think about it...

When someone visits your website, they also have lots of other tabs open. We're going to discuss this in the final chapter of this book, but when they are checking out your website, you're one of lots of other options available to them.

There's lots of noise.

When they see your post on social media, they are busy scrolling and at the same time the channel is putting other posts, ads, and other things in the way.

There's lots of noise.

When they see your listing on an OTA, the OTA is actively recommending other properties and locations to the user.

There's lots of noise.

When they view your Google Business listing, again Google is recommending you to go and check out other locations similar.

You guessed it, there's lots of noise.

With an email, you have the one on one attention of the reader.

If you write and craft your email correctly, they will consume that email in full.

There's no noise.

But, the trouble is this:

99% of hospitality owners I come across do this wrong.

Guess who the 1% are?

You're right...

#TeamBoostly members.

The reason why people don't like email marketing is that they look at their own inbox and see all the pointless garbage that sits in there. Companies and businesses who treat an email list as a reason to bombard the reader with emails that look like glossy magazine ads.

It's time to shift your mindset with emails.

It's time I share with you my secret sauce that I have mastered not only for The Grainary, but Boostly, and now taught to over 1000 hosts around the world.

Not only that, but I'm going to give you a template that you can copy, paste, amend, personalise, and send out to your new email list at the end of this chapter.

You need to head to bookdirectplaybook.com to get this.

Hosts who I have helped crack this marketing actively attribute so many of their direct bookings to this.

I get messages and see posts in the Boostly Academy Group all the time they go along the lines of:

> 'I sent out an email to my list this weekend and I had X amount of enquiries and X amount of new direct bookings!'

There are many tools, softwares, and websites that provide a service to help you with this.

And I'm going to leave a resources list at bookdirectplaybook.com

However, just like social media, I know that websites, services, and offerings will adapt and change over the years.

I want this book to be as evergreen as possible and to be as relevant now as it will be in 5 or 10 years time.

So, what I'm going to do is explain the key fundamentals to email marketing and then, on the companion course, I'll show you a few things to do and give you the template I mentioned for you to put into practice in the GID session.

Okay, let's begin.

HOW TO GET STARTED

When you think of email marketing and sending a thousand people an email, what's the first thought that goes through your mind?

That's a lot of emails?!

Or at least that's what I assume.

So, what if I was to tell you that there is software out there that will send your email out en masse and all you need to do is send it once?

What if I also told you that the same software will personalise the email for you so it makes the reader think you're manually sending out the email to them like a much loved pen pal?

Sounds better, right?

Well, this software is here and, even better news, it is free to get started.

I have left a full list of resources of websites over on bookdirectplaybook. com which are free to get started and when you grow, they will grow with you and charge a small monthly fee.

Please let me tell you, whatever charge they give you will be worth it.

Always think if I get ONE booking this month because of these emails then thats an excellent return on investment.

To give you an example, I spend $200 a month for the email marketing service I use.

The return on my investment is 200% what I spend on it.

I believe so much in this marketing channel that I have slowly, over the years, increased the amount I spend on it. And I will continue to do so for years to come.

What you need to get started is an Email Marketing Service.

Again, I have provided a full updated list on the companion course bookdirectplaybook.com

Once you have created your system, you need to set it up.

You will add in your email address.

This is key

Do not use a generic personal email account here (i.e. gmail). You'll need your own business domain, for example: mark@boostly.co.uk. This shows you are a professional outfit and not a scammer.

Emails work exactly the same as social media, there's an algorithm. With trillions of emails being sent everyday, our inboxes are getting busier and busier. The big email companies have implemented algorithms to make sure that the reader doesn't have to be bombarded with spam and junk. The best way to avoid this, and to get your email into the reader's inbox, is to get a business domain email.

It's simple enough and costs very little a month to activate. Head to your hosting company where your website domain is and ask them to set it up.

What you need to do now is to create a signup form so people can sign up to your email list.

Every Email Marketing Service is different in how they do this, so what you need to do is access the tutorial section of the service you went with.

What's key here is to make sure your sign up form is compliant to the laws in your country. In Europe they have GDPR for example. You don't want to be getting on the wrong side of the law, as the fines are heavy. The best and easiest way to protect yourself is to make sure that everyone who signs up to your email list has ticked a little box to give you permission to send them emails.

The main mistake that people make at this point is that they upload a large list of previous customers and guests to their email database assuming that they can do this without getting permission.

Please don't do this.

If you haven't had an email marketing service in the past and this is the first time you are doing so, let's start from scratch.

Once you have created your list and you have set up a sign up form, you're now good to go in and do the next stage which is setup tags. Tagging is crucial for email marketing because it's going to be the main way to segment your list.

Now, if I have lost you at tagging and segmenting, then head over to Bookdirectplaybook.com for a video where I show you exactly what I mean.

Let's recap:

You have created your FREE account.

You have created your FREE sign up form.

You have setup tags and segments for FREE.

The final thing to do is to create email automations.

Email automations are fantastic and I love them. When set up correctly, it's the equivalent of hiring a 24 hour salesperson.

Email automations work in many ways, but the best way, and the way

I like to set them up, is when you have someone sign up to your email list.

The user will receive a few emails that will look to turn them from a looker into a booker. If you're thinking that you haven't got a clue on what to write and put into here...never fear! The email template that I said I had created for you takes care of this. It's called the Looker into a Booker template. Emails that you can copy, paste, personalise, and load into your automation right now.

Head over to bookdirectplaybook.com and you can go and grab it today for (you guessed it) free!

Congratulations, you have now gone and set up the core basics of your Email Marketing Service.

Now it's time to go and get people onto your email list.

HOW TO GROW YOUR EMAIL LIST

The best way to start this is to add your sign up form link to the following places:

YOUR WEBSITE

The amount of people who visit your website and will take action and book there and then is very low.

The trick here is to keep them in your world and to get them on to your email list now so they don't leave and forget you.

The text you use here is crucial.

If you say the word 'newsletter' at any point, you might as well not bother.

I can't think of anything more off putting that saying:

'Join my newsletter'

It screams **'I don't know what I am talking about.'**

So, promise me this, don't call it that.

Instead, think of something that your ideal guest would like to click on and give up their email address in return for.

For example:

If you look at the Boostly website, it says:

Boost Your Direct Bookings with 5 Short Videos

Claim your FREE Online Video Training
that has helped over 100,000 hospitality
owners and property managers worldwide,
to skyrocket their bookings!

It's slightly different to a newsletter.

Bringing it back to hospitality, one of the best email lists I am on is Jayne Hancock's from Field's Lodge B&B in Pembrokeshire, UK.

Go and check out her email sign up form wording:

fieldslodge.co.uk

Free Guide Reveals…

Where to go and what to do in Pembrokeshire:

- The best beaches to visit

- All you need to know about visiting Skomer Island

- What not to miss

It attracts you in and focuses on the customer avatar.

Now, at this point please don't go and copy mine or Jayne's. Get inspired and think of what you can write on your website that will get the user to take action.

If you want to share your ideas and brainstorm, come into the Hospitality Community Facebook Group and post up what you're thinking. We have over 6000 hosts in there who will be able to help and share their advice.

After you have added your sign up form link to your website, let's head over to your social media channels.

The easiest way to grow your list is to post up that you would like to stay in touch via email.

Again, when you post up on socials, don't say:

'Join my email newsletter.'

Instead, focus on what you think someone would join.

Jayne could put:

> 'Hey all, I have been busy creating a full list of places to visit in the local area.
>
> These are not only my favourite places to go to, but all of our guests from over the years. If you would like to get a copy, head to {INSERT WEB LINK]}.'

You will be pleasantly surprised at how many people will head over and give up their email address for this.

Finally, let's focus on your previous guests.

You can't add all of these email lists to your email marketing software without getting permission. However, this doesn't mean you can't get in touch and let them know how they can keep in touch.

Just please make sure that when you do this don't make it copy and paste.

Personalise it!

Yes this is going to be time consuming, so what I recommend is apply the 80/20 rule.

Go through all of your guests from the past year and find the 20% of your guests who brought you 80% of the most joy, liked, or even bought in the most revenue.

You work out whatever your 80/20 rule is and send them a personalised email.

If you would rather not email because you're wary or nervous around your email laws, then send a voice note or text message. Failing that, send them a nice letter in the post.

Every booking from here on in will be giving you this information at the point of booking, so you have it to use to remarket to via email for years to come.

GET IT DONE

Okay, lots to take on here.

I have laid out the exact system you need to get started with email marketing and even provided you with the template.

What I want for you to do is to get setup.

It's free and easy to do, all you need to do is take action.

Box if off in your calendar.

Get into a quiet room and get it done.

When you have, I have homework for you.

Send me via Instagram @boostlyuk the link to your sign up form.

Tell me that you have come from this book and I will check it out.

I love seeing the Boostly emails in the wild and working.

Who knows, you might turn me from a Looker into a Booker for a future stay!

Go and get it done!

THE
BOOK DIRECT
PLAYBOOK

HOW TO MAKE THE OTAS WORK FOR YOU

I can already anticipate the comments, messages, and reactions to including a chapter on Online Travel Agents (OTAs) in a book all about increasing direct bookings.

And look, I get it, it's my fault.

For years I have been preaching the #BookDirect movement.

However, people misinterpret my message, as I am not for one minute saying you need to delete your listings off the big OTA websites. That would be business suicide. The amount of money they spend in advertising and brand recognition is crazy levels. It would be crazy to not have a presence on there.

No, what I am saying is this:

Make the OTAs work for you, not the other way round.

In this chapter I am going to explore this, change your mindset, and try to explain how you need to see it as a marketing channel, not the be all and end all.

I am going to show you some easy tactics and tips you can implement into your business to make a start.

There is going to be GID sessions and, of course, I will have video tutorials available over on bookdirectplaybook.com.

Airbnb is not the be all and end all in your business model. You cannot think they are looking out for you.

Now they have joined the likes of Booking Holiday and Expedia group on the stock market, their core focus is their shareholders.

Not you.

It is not the same company which was started up by three chaps looking to cover rent in San Francisco. It's much more than that now. You cannot rely on that one platform to bring in your bookings.

Do not build your house on someone else's land.

And look, if you're just looking to do this on the side and it's more of a hobby than a business, fair enough.

There are some fantastic Airbnb focused books that you can check out. My friend Danny Rusteen has one of the best Airbnb books on the market, *Optimize Your Bnb*. Danny is an ex-Airbnb employee and only focuses on that platform.

This book; this is for those who want to build a business.

And I am here to tell you, you do not build your house on someone else's land.

I know hosts who did this, and I saw what happened to them in March 2020 when Airbnb, without warning, let all of their guests cancel free of charge, with no fees to pay and without any regard to their cancellation policy.

I knew hosts who relied on 95% of their bookings coming from Airbnb who lost their businesses.

I tried to warn them.

But it was too late.

This is why you need to change your mindset.

Airbnb, the Booking Holidays Group, Expedia Group and all of their associated websites and businesses should be used as a marketing channel.

Treat them like social media channels.

I feel that 80% of the people who have picked up this book to read will be on the same page as me. However this is talking to the other 20%. This little section is for you.

In this chapter, and in this book, I am going to not only change your mindset on this, but also make you more money per booking.

Imagine having a booking where it comes in and you're in total control.

You have all of the guests' data, you have the power of the cancellation policies, and you can have clear contact pre and post stay without any influence from a third party.

That's what you get with a direct booking.

Let me stress...this is not all about money.

There are services you can use where you pay a 'finders fee' or 'commission' but the booking is still yours.

That's a direct booking.

Any booking that comes in and you have total control of it.

That's a direct booking.

Now that we have ticked off this box, let's get stuck into some actionable tips you can do right now to make a start. We're going to begin on the best tactic to convert an OTA booking into a direct one.

THE EASIEST WAY TO CONVERT AN OTA BOOKING INTO A DIRECT ONE

This section will, I know, cause a few messages in my inbox. I'm fully aware of this.

But it works.

It works because I have used it and coached hundreds of other hosts how to utilise it.

And before you ask me, yes, it is allowed.

And no, it does not affect your search algorithm.

It's all about incentivising your guests.

The good news is it will take 30 minutes to implement and you can sit and forget it.

What I am going to show you is how you can convert a booking from an OTA into a direct booking. For full context, for this to work at it's finest you need a Property Management Software in place. If you haven't got one, head to Boostly.co.uk/pms and pick one. Go and set it up and come back to the book.

For those who already have a PMS setup, read on.

As you know, when a booking comes in your PMS kicks into gear and sends out an automated email to the guest.

One of my big pet peeves is when hosts say 'why should we try and take on Booking.com and Expedia? The guests are too loyal to them and will always book there.'

NOT TRUE.

The guest is only loyal to one person, and that's them. If they knew that they could get a better deal elsewhere, they would book there.

The reason why hosts assume this is because they are not marketing their business correctly.

I have stated so many times:

> 'Why would a guest book with you directly
> if you fail to explain the benefits of booking
> direct at every stage of the booking process.'

More on the booking process in the final chapter in this book.

Even if a guest books via an OTA, there is a chance to convert it to a direct booking. And again, it's all about presenting the facts to a guest at every stage.

I think I've teased you enough about this, let's delve in.

Of course, I have created a tutorial video showing you exactly how to do this on bookdirectplaybook.com

Here's what to do:

Go into your PMS email templates.

You're going to look for the template that goes to the guest after the point of booking. What we're going to do here is customise it.

However, before we do that, let's talk about your check-in process.

Now, we all assume that the only way we're going to get a guest to book direct is talk about the 'rates'.

BEST RATE WHEN YOU BOOK DIRECT

This is the common phrase I see bounded around.

Now, let's not assume our guest only cares about money. Yes, money is important and people love to save money, but I'll tell you what else they like:

Incentives.

All you need to do here is have a look at what the big chains are doing in your country.

Go and look at their websites.

Look at the incentives you get when you book direct:

- Free WiFi

- Earlier check in

- Later check out

- Free breakfast

Now, why aren't we doing the same?

I'm not for one minute saying go and offer breakfasts when you don't offer them already. I'm not even going to say to push yourself to get the cleaning done quicker.

Here's what I am saying...

Let's say your check in time is 1pm.

Do this:

Keep your check in time at 1pm. Then go to your Online Travel Agents extranet and move the check in time to 5 pm.

And this is what you're going to do to remind the guest.

In the email template that goes out, the wording will structure like this:

Hi {GUEST NAME}

Thank you for your booking with us.

This quick email is confirmation and includes some important information about your stay so please make sure you read to the end.

Date of Arrival

Date of checkout

Important check-in time information:

If you have booked your stay with us directly (i.e. via our website, email, or phone call) your check in time is **1 pm.**

Note: make sure you really emphasis this bit.

If you have booked your stay with us via a third party (i.e. Booking.com, Airbnb, Expedia) your check in time is **5 pm.**

If you would like to discuss anything about your stay or make any changes with us here's our direct line to contact us {INSERT PHONE NUMBER}.

Have a great day,

{YOUR NAME}

Let's delve into the psychological aspect of this.

What you're doing here is punishing people for booking via a third party. Think about this from their point of view. And if you have children, or ever had to fly to a destination to get to your property, think about that too.

You've had to travel for a few hours. Then you get to the destination and you can't get in your property until 5 pm.

If they had booked with you directly they could get the incentive.

Depending on how brave you are as well, you can go further on and mention that if they have booked directly they will get a Welcome Hamper, Late Checkout, Free WiFi etc.

Again, this is optional, but the more you can twist the incentive edge, the more chance you have of the next bit working.

What you find is that the person reading this wants the incentives but they were unaware of them.

So, they will call you.

Then it's a case of you keeping a cool head and this will work every time.

The guest will call and ask about an earlier check in time and other incentives.

All you have to say is:

'Yes, of course, all we need to do is get your email address to confirm for security reasons.' (Because you know that the OTAs don't pass you their real email address.) And then ask for them to confirm their card details they want the payment to go from.

Then the next bit is key.

'Thank you, all you need to do now is go to the dashboard of the platform you booked on and cancel your stay.

There will be no cancellation charges.

We will take care of everything for you and swap it over to a direct booking where you will get {INSERT INCENTIVES} and send you a new email confirmation.'

They are none the wiser.

They just care about the incentives.

They don't know that the OTAs charge you a commission.

You get the direct booking and this is the best bit:

IT HAS ZERO EFFECT OR COME BACK ON YOU.

1 | It does NOT have any impact on your algorithm and search results.

Because it is the guest who cancels and NOT you, so the OTAs are treating this like any other cancellation.

What's important is that you NEVER cancel a booking. You might as well delete your account if you're going to cancel a booking.

2 | There is no comeback from the OTAs

Again, because you have not contacted the guest directly and demanded they cancel the booking, you're not breaking any Terms and Conditions here. The guest is the one who cancelled the booking.

YOU GET THE BOOKING.

YOU GET THE DATA.

YOU GET IT ON YOUR TERMS.

YOU GET TO POCKET THE COMMISSION THAT WOULD HAVE GONE TO THE OTA.

And the guest is happy because they get the incentives.

Clever right?

Now for a GID session. Go and implement this into your business, test it for 90 days.

I can't wait to see your results.

CLOSE OUT YOUR CALENDAR TO THE OTAS

One thing that has always amazed me is how many of our juicy dates we give away to the OTAs.

What do I mean by this?

Well, you can now look in your calendar for the next 12 months. I guarantee you there will be dates in the next 12 months that you could sell two or three times over.

This could be a local event or a national holiday, you know what I'm talking about. I know you're thinking about at least one right now.

Okay, so tell me, why are you listing these dates on the OTAs?

Why are you giving them the date?

Why aren't you saving it for yourself?

Now is the time to remind you of how incredibly useful your PMS and channel managers are.

The problem is that you're likely not using them to their fullest advantage. You're not alone here, the majority of hosts use their PMS providers as tools to push rates onto (because that's what they're mainly marketed for).

However, we're going to mix things up a little. The first thing I want you to do is go into your PMS and channel manager and close off the important dates to the OTAs and any third party.

Remember, this isn't set in stone. It's not like you're advertising in the newspaper or magazine. You can change as you go. That's the beauty of the internet and modern day integrations.

You can make a change and it's actioned within seconds. So you can afford to be super confident with your new marketing decisions.

Next up, try this...

Send out an email to your list. Explain that there are some key dates in the future that are only bookable directly via you. And list them off.

Make very clear that it's a 'first come first served basis' and if anyone wants to book they can call you directly or visit your website's online booking engine.

By offering something that is 'exclusive' (and of great value to your guests), you'll see your direct bookings rise, notably. Try and execute this strategy every 3 months and you'll see the results for yourself.

Not only will the profits start rolling in, but by having these dates booked in advance, you'll have more time to plan and strategise around your calendar, and run your business more efficiently.

MAKE THEM WORK FOR YOU, NOT THE OTHER WAY AROUND

HOW TO MAKE SURE YOU NEVER WASTE YOUR MONEY ON PAID LISTING WEBSITES

Before the commission model became popular in the world of hospitality by the big OTAs, the way to advertise your business was in magazines or online listing websites.

It's now very rare to find listing websites that charge a listing fee, however there are some great ones out there that are very niche.

Remember, in the customer avatar training I demonstrated how to be present in all the places that your Future Potential Guests are? Well, this little section links back to that, beautifully.

The following tactic is something I have practiced for years now and it ensures that I always get the most of my money with a paid listing website.

Now, the majority of the time you'll be cold approached by these websites, at which point, I advise you do the following. First up, ask the paid listing website for two businesses who have benefited from their service.

Then, visit the website for yourself and find a provider from your area, county, or state that is paying to be listed with them. Once you've done this, call these businesses up and ask for an honest opinion.

The thing is, the recommendations you'll have received from the paid listing website themselves will be their readymade case studies anyway (so they're bound to be positive). Which is why you need to do your own research and get a well-balanced opinion.

This way, you're far more likely to make a better, well-informed decision for yourself and your business.

At the end of the day, if you implement the tactic I demonstrated about making sure you're 'appearing everywhere', and in the most important places, and if said listing site comes up organically off the back of a search engine search, then the SEO value in itself is great.

I would also keep active and ontop of the listing sites as soon as you're signed up. It's best to cover all bases here.

If this works and starts to bring in more booking enquiries for you, then see what else you could do to advertise more with your chosen service provider. Here are some options of potential extras:

A banner ad on the top of their website.

Email newsletter mention.

Editorial write up on your properties and business.

GOOGLE IS THE NEXT BIG OTA

Google is bound to disrupt the travel industry.

It's already dabbled. In fact, it's actively dabbling at the point of writing this book, and it's only going to become more powerful.

It's only a matter of time for Google, and depending on when you pick up this book, it'll be 'pre' or 'post' their ultimate takeover. There's simply no denying it.

The most important takeaway from this section is to think of Google as your homepage.

Take advantage of all of the features it offers you.

To help you out, I'm going to list them here and then create tutorial videos on the free companion course on bookdirectplaybook.com where I'll continue to update as Google expands its reach.

The main features to take advantage of in Google are:

- Google Business Listing

- Google Analytics

- Google Site Console

- Google Adwords

- Google Vacation Rentals

Again, I will cover all these in more detail on the free companion course and show you how to implement each into your business.

My prediction is that Google itself will go in competition with the major OTAs; and I wouldn't be surprised at all to see Expedia Group, Booking Holidays Group, and Airbnb pull away from relying on Google search to drive traffic to their websites.

For now though, open a browser on your computer and go into private mode.

Then run a search for YOUR BUSINESS NAME in LOCATION and see what results Google gives.

What you're looking for is:

1 | Which websites come up at the top of the search? Is it yours or an OTAs?

2 | Does your business come up in the map results?

3 | Where does your website come up in the search results?

4 | How many times does your website or social media results come up in the first page of Google?

What you're trying to work out is how Google presents your business to a Future Potential Guest.

Then head to the bookdirectplaybook.com to work on fixes and how to make sure your business is at as many touch points as possible.

Now, let's tie this all together and then have one grand final Get it Done Session before becoming winners.

This is it.

The final chapter of the book.

This is where we tie everything we have learnt together and put it into practice in the real world. This is where you transform your business into a direct booking machine and I'm so excited to see the results.

When I first started teaching and coaching hospitality owners, I posted a few articles on the Boostly website. I wanted to create 5 articles to document what I had studied, practiced, and mastered for the family business.

One of the core reasons why we were able to increase our bookings and achieve so many 5 star reviews, and cut down massively on cancellations, was driven by one process.

It's one now, to the day, I talk about, but still so many hosts don't understand.

To guide you through this, I have updated the training for this book and there is also a video explanation in the free companion course showing specific parts to look for in your business and how to make sure you're avoiding what so many other hosts fall for.

This process is, of course, the **Guest Booking Process.**

There are actually 5 stages to the guest booking process:

1 | Plan

2 | Research

3 | Decide

4 | Book

5 | Buyer's Remorse

In this chapter I am going to lay out each section and give you actionable pieces of advice on how you can master each one, so you guide your Future Potential Guest smoothly from Looker to Booker without any barriers blocking your way.

There will be mini Get it Done Sessions thrown in for good measure (you've had loads of practice already, you'll be great).

Let's begin.

THE GUEST BOOKING PROCESS

1. PLAN

When the average booker comes to this stage of their journey, they will begin at the same place.

Google.

Good old, trusty Google.

Whether they're booking a stay for themselves, or somebody else, a Google search is the most likely place they'll begin.

We can safely assume that they're at the very first step of their guest booking journey, the planning.

They might know where they want to travel to in terms of location, but they'll be open to options for the specific type of accommodation. This is great because this is your golden opportunity to ensure that you're making yourself visible to them, your customer avatar(s).

If you've skimmed past the Customer Avatar Chapter in this Playbook, I recommend you go and check it out, because I've laid out exactly what you need to do there to master the planning stage of the guest booking process.

You need to be wherever your Future Potential Guest is.

Your name, your brand, your image, needs to be in clear sight of wherever your FPG goes and hangs out.

BE EVERYWHERE.

It's a tactic that is applied by big brands and they spend millions to do so.

The big brands will spend millions in advertising and marketing to make sure that when you're ready to make a purchase, your eyes fall onto their brand first. As if by magic (but it's not actually magic, it's very smart and very strategic planning).

Take, for example:

- TV
- Radio
- Print
- Google Ads
- Facebook Ads
- Billboards

You name it, they advertise on it, to appeal to your subconscious mind. Ever heard of the business saying 'Rent a place in your customers' minds?' Well, that's exactly what these industry giants are doing.

I cannot tell you how powerful top-of-the-mind advertising is.

And before you argue:

'Mark, I haven't got the money to do this?!'

I should tell you that you really ought to trust me by now, because there's an easy way of doing this, all while spending mere pennies in the process.

It's all been clearly laid out for you in the Customer Avatar Chapter, where we've really hit home on how you need to be hanging out where your ideal guests hang out (and making yourself known in the process). It's about making sure that you are present wherever your ideal guests are searching - just before they're ready to make that direct booking with you.

I've also pointed out in the OTA chapter about Google and how it's going to be the next online travel agency and how you have to make sure you treat a Google search as your homepage.

Okay, so right now there will be two types of Future Potential Guests at the planning stage:

1 | People who don't know who you are

2 | People who know who you are

The people who know who you are fall into the following categories:

1 | People who have stayed with you before

2 | People who have heard about you from a recommendation

The first is simple, but it's something that so many get wrong, and actually, if you've ever had a guest repeat-book with you via an Online Travel Agent, then this is what you're doing wrong.

Just because a guest has stayed with you before, it doesn't mean they remember everything about you. Please don't assume this to be the case. We cannot be so naive.

I mean, try and remember a place you stayed with for the first time over the past 6 months. Unless you have been following them on social media or receiving emails from them, I guarantee you won't remember the host's name or their website.

And it's the same with your guests.

So, the top tips here from me are:

1 | Stay Top of Mind. Do not go quiet on social media or email marketing. This is why it is so important to be posting daily and sending emails at least once a month to your email list.

2 | Make sure that when a guest searches for your business on Google, your website is the first thing they see.

Now, the problem with the latter is that the OTAs know that a large majority of people will search for your business on Google. It's called **bidding on your brand name.**

And before you think 'Can they even do that?'

The answer is, yes. Unfortunately.

When you sign the Ts&Cs to join their website, you give them the authority to do so. It's a clause in the contract that we don't often read, and while it's sneaky, I'm here to show you how to fight fire with fire.

Basically, we need you to bid on your own brand name on Google. It's so powerful and has saved hosts I know thousands of pounds in commission costs over the years.

Now, I could write a whole book on this topic alone because it has a very detailed explanation. So, instead I've recorded a tutorial video over on bookdirectplaybook.com where you can follow along and set it up in less than 30 minutes.

The whole point of this section is that you get everywhere for your ideal guest. If they don't go directly to your website and they go to an OTA or another website, then they at least still get exposed to your brand and your business.

GET IT DONE

You're going to go to and run a search to make sure you're listed and visible on the 20% of the searches that come up 80% of the time (remember that grand 80/20 rule?).

You're also going to set up a **Bid on Brand Strategy** with **Google Ads.**

All the help and guidance is on bookdirectplaybook. com and I've outlined it all in layman's terms.

As soon as you've done this, return to this section of the Playbook and continue.

If you have any questions, please reach out via Instagram and send a message @boostlyuk.

2. RESEARCH

This next step of the Guest Booking Process is where you have to make sure you're 'clickable'.

Trendy word. But what do I mean by that?

This is where your branding and photos, as well as how you appeal to your Future Potential Guest, is important. How you present yourself online here will win or lose a booking. Get this wrong, and your FPG will go elsewhere.

First up, what's important is that your main photo is the same on all of the listing websites. Brand recognition is key and any features that are key to your business and brand need to be showing up here.

For example, at The Grainary, where I grew up, we were famous for having Highland Cows. If you've never seen a Highland Cow before, go and run a search on the internet. They are stunning, long-haired cows, and were extremely popular. We used to have people come and visit us specifically for the Highland Cows.

It therefore made sense for our main photo on all of the OTAs and listing websites to be the famous Highland Cows in the foreground, with our main building and lake area in the background. A stunning shot.

What's best was that it was instantly recognisable, never mind which platforms the guests were searching from.

For those of you who feel that you don't have any distinguishing features, get creative and make them.

For example, in city centre apartments where all the buildings are the same - focus on your interiors. What can you do to have the brand name stand out?

I saw a fantastic example by Shamil Mae who's based in Birmingham, UK.

He has a luxury range of apartments in Birmingham and the brand name is Maevela®. Mae has decorated the apartment and in the units he has wall decorations spelling out the brand name. It looks amazing and the brand name stands out whenever you see his units online.

Go and check out what he's doing, it'll really help with the inspiration.

He's also a great follow on Instagram and is super talented:

@maevela_

While we're talking about photos, please, at this point let's all agree on one thing: you need to hire a professional to take your photos. Remember, we've covered this in the earlier section of this Playbook.

Unless you're reading this and you're a professional photographer yourself, or have a close contact who is, then you'll need to invest in this.

Please don't do it yourself.

Please don't do what my Dad used to do at The Grainary. He would walk around our B&B with his camera phone in hand. He would proudly walk into the room, plug his phone into the computer and declare:

> 'Mark, I have new photos!'

I always used to humour him and say, 'yes Dad, thanks.' I've already briefly mentioned this in the book, but there's such a big lesson to learn here.

Rather than using my lovely father's photos, I was instantly putting them in the recycle bin and messaging my friend who was a professional to please get up to the farm ASAP. Trust me, it was for the good of our family business.

The trouble is, many people at this point assume they are going to have to spend thousands on a professional photoshoot. And I guess this could be the case in an ordinary world.

But luckily, I have your back as always, and Boostly's world is far from ordinary.

There's a wicked training session on bookdirectplaybook.com, where I've shown you how to bag a professional photoshoot for free. I'll assume you're going to head off and get this sorted now, so we can move onto the next part:

What's important now is the layout.

Let's first focus on the OTAs that you're listed on.

Just because they let you upload hundreds of photos, doesn't mean you have to.

Remember:

LESS IS MORE

The most important photos for you will be the first 6; and a heads up, you should use no more than 20. More than 20 is overkill.

If you overwhelm your Future Potential Guest they will leave.

IF YOU CONFUSE YOU LOSE

When you're laying out your photos, you want to act like you're telling a story and walking a Future Potential Guest through your property. And whatever you do, make sure you use the captions in each photo to explain exactly what they're saying. Leaving room for guessing is a dangerous game.

For example:

The first one will be the USP - The Unique Selling Photo - as I've referred to in the earlier part of this Playbook. So, this would be your version of the Highland Cow.

Then the second photo will be an interior shot of the feature place of your property.

The next one will lead on from that, and you explain the captions as you go.

To reiterate, the reason why the photos are so important is that once guests have clicked on your listing, it's the first place they go to. They don't read the descriptions, they get excited by flash photography, and merrily hop on over to that first.

A photo is worth 1000 thousand words and in hospitality it couldn't be closer to the truth.

'But Mark, how am I going to get this right?'

The only way to do this is test.

There's a fantastic website called usertesting.com and you can hire people to give feedback on your websites and listing websites. I use this a lot and they give valuable insight and feedback for a very low price.

Tweak and test, you'll never get it right first time.

The same goes for your website.

I explained more about this in the website chapter, but you have to make sure that the first thing they see is:

- Your USP photo

- Your tagline/headline

The whole point of this is that you want to make your business sticky. You want to get someone to land on your website or your listing website and want to stick around to find out more.

And for those who land on your social media page to do the research, again, make sure it is sticky.

Go and tidy the social channels up and make sure it is obvious who you are, what you do, who you serve and how they can book.

Please don't be naive enough to think that at this stage you're the only business that the Future Potential Guest is checking out here. The average user will have multiple tabs open at this point and will be delving further through the decision making process.

The question you need to be asking is this:

Am I speaking to my ideal guest? My customer avatar?

And if you don't know what that means at this stage, then go and revisit the Customer Avatar chapter as that will give you all the clarification you need.

When you crack that chapter, this whole section is so much easier.

GET IT DONE

I want you to go to everywhere you're listed on and your website and do a proper audit of what you're doing and how you're speaking and presenting your business online.

The questions to ask:

1 | Who is my customer avatar?

2 | Who am I appealing to?

3 | Are my photos a true representation of the business and the property?

4 | Is the wording I use speaking to my customer avatar?

Maybe you will need to outsource and bring in a professional photographer and copywriter.

I can guarantee you one thing...

The return on investment on outsourcing and hiring on those two at this stage will be untold.

If you get this part right, you will have people demanding to stay with you.

You will be booked up beyond belief.

So much so, you will be generating extra revenue working with other hosts and passing them bookings in your area because you're so over booked.

3.DECIDE

Let's quickly recap what we have done so far.

We've made sure that our business and brand is everywhere to be seen, where our ideal guest is going to be looking, thanks to learning some of the tactics the massive corporations spend millions trying to work out.

We have then covered how to make sure our business stands out so it gets the click and makes us more sticky to our Future Potential Guest.

Right now, if done correctly, we should be in the final choices of the Future Potential Guest.

At this stage, you will be a saved link, a bookmark, or have been sent an email to check if it's okay to book.

It's what you do here that's key to getting to the next stage.

Quite simply, the goal here is to knock down as many potential barriers to the Future Potential Guest as they will have put up. And it doesn't matter if this is on the OTA sites or on your own website.

This is where you will have to look locally and see what everyone is offering and doing.

When everyone is zigging, can you zag?

And this isn't something you can set and forget. This is where you will have to check in once a quarter to keep tabs.

For example, if everyone is running a strict cancellation policy, can you be flexible?

If everyone has the same layout and decor as you, what can you do differently to stand out?

It's going to be different for everyone reading this book and it really narrows the focus down to you and your local area.

What I want to stress here is that it is NOT a price thing. I don't want for you to feel like you have to race to the bottom.

I would never advise to do that.

You need to have your price point and be confident to stick with it.

Instead, it's really important at this stage to really put yourself in the mindset of your ideal guest and what they would be looking for so that they will see you as their best option for their stay.

Whatever you decide on, you need to be shouting about it so it is clear.

Again, don't overcomplicate it.

If your customer avatar is people who travel with pets, and you decide to provide a free pet bed, provide pet snacks, and don't charge any extra for the cleaning cost and to have the pet stay with them, you need to state this either on your website or the description of your listing.

I would also be talking about this on your social media pages.

Do not think that your Future Potential Guest at this point hasn't run a search on Google or has gone to find you on social media to find out more about you.

And as we state in the website chapter, it is crucial that you get your social proof visible on your homepage here. Have you won any awards recently? Again, explain about this. Have you got a service set up where the guest is covered for damages and breakages without any cost as part of their stay? Talk and show this off.

If you never talk about this, the guest will never know about it.

Again, don't go on and on and on about how good you are. You need to focus on the things that matter to your customer avatar.

The way that hosts go wrong here is they are either too shy to talk about it or they babble on and on and bore the guest.

What you will find is that the majority of the time, you have already won over the person doing the research, but here the key thing is to convince the person or people they are travelling with.

You need to make it so simple for the person doing the research to explain to the other people in the party and for them to go:

HELL YEAH!

You're always striving for the **HELL YEAH.**

Because if it isn't a **HELL YEAH**, it's normally a **no.**

GET IT DONE

What I want you to do here is to go over all of the benefits for people booking with you. Get out a pen and paper and brain dump it on to the pad.

Then, what I want you to do is go through your website and your listing websites and honestly assess whether you're talking about this clearly and precisely to your Future Potential Guest.

If not, then make the changes.

When you have made the changes to your business, send me a DM on Instagram with the links to your website and listing websites and state what the main benefits of booking with you are and I will be happy to check for you.

4.BOOK

I am often asked:

'Which is the most important step in the booking process?'

I have thought long and hard about this, and I have to say it is this one.

Unfortunately, this is the ONE step where you can't 100% influence the outcome.

The quality of your online booking engine will largely determine whether you get that booking, or not. Ultimately, the entire process hangs with its bare hands on this part.

You may well have invested time and money and effort into the other stages of the booking process, as well as done all of the work to not only stand out, but convince the Future Potential Guest that you are the host that they should stay with.

Of the thousands of other options, you have shined the brightest and built that connection with your ideal guest. At which point, they have visited your website with their paying card in-hand to complete the booking...and then, guess what?

Your PMS and their online booking engine has let you down.

It's a shame, but I've seen it so many times. Let me tell you about this one particular occasion.

There's a Story Behind Every Booking

A good friend of mine posted on her social media page:

'I am trying to book a Christmas break for me and my friends and I am here with my card attempting to give a hospitality owner some money for a big booking. But their website is awful. I cannot make this booking!'

And she posted this to her massive social media following.

I'm not going to name and shame the property she was trying to book with.

But do you know what she then did? She went and found them on Booking.com and booked there instead. The property hosts would've been kicking themselves at this stage.

Sadly, my friend isn't alone.

If a Future Potential Guest has a bad user experience on your website they will leave. FACT!

And when they leave, they don't come back, based on their user experience.

If you're thinking right now:

'I wonder what my booking process is like on my website?'

Then please stop reading this book and go and test it now.

And also, don't just test it on your computer, go and test it on your phone as well.

I urge you to please, honestly, assess what it is like:

- How much friction is there?

- Is it hard to enter in your name and personal details?

- Is it clear which sections you need to click on, and what kind of information website visitors need to provide?

- How simple is your online booking engine making it for a guest to provide card details?

- Do you have to pinch the phone to zoom in?

- Are the buttons large enough?

These are all the questions that should be going through your thought process. Learn from my friend's story.

And remember this...

If at any point you're struggling to navigate across your own website, then you can guarantee that your Future Potential Guests will be, too.

So, if the latter applies to you and you've just realised that your website doesn't run like clockwork, there's no need to panic and think all is lost, then this is where Boostly can help.

Our API technology links directly with your Property Management Software so your future potential guest can book directly on your website.

To truly build your house on your own land, you need to make sure you have a website that has the power of Airbnb.

Visit boostly.co.uk/website to see real world examples of a powerful direct bookings website in action.

5.BUYER'S REMORSE

Once again, **congratulations!**

You have the booking.

Let's do a little celebration dance shall we...

The 'Booking Boogie', as I like to call it.

You've managed to stand out, convince your guest that you're the right one for them, and knock over any final hurdles and answer questions that have made it easier to complete a direct booking.

Usually, at this point I see so many hosts fail.

A simple lack of communication is often the main contributor towards a cancellation.

Of course, I should stress that it is very rare to find anyone in the world of hospitality who has a 0% cancellation rate. But you can dramatically reduce the amount of cancellations you have and that's through one tactic that works time and time again.

It's simple to do.
It costs nothing.
And the return on investment is invaluable.

This one little tweak in your business could result in 5 or 6 figure bumps in your revenue...

And this one thing will dramatically increase the ratio of fantastic reviews you get online and the amount of raving super fans you create off the back of it.

By now, you're probably itching to know what it is, right? Well, here it is:

PICK UP YOUR PHONE AND SPEAK WITH YOUR GUEST

If this is going to be you, or a member of your team, or even a future team member, when the booking comes in, grab your phone and either:

A | Give them a call

B | Send a text message

You will be amazed at what happens next.

Use the below as sort of a loose script:

> 'Hey {FIRST NAME}, it's {YOUR NAME} from {YOUR BUSINESS}.
>
> I'm calling to say thank you for confirming your reservation with us.
>
> Quick question...

Then you can use any one of these open ended questions:

- What brings you to the area?

- Why are you coming to {INSERT TOWN}?

- What is the nature of your trip?

- What made you book with us?

- How can I make your stay extra special?

The questions are endless, but if you have never done this before, give it a go.

I guarantee you with everything I know, I preach and do this because it will have a fantastic impact on your business. More importantly, it will massively cut down on your cancellations.

Now, before I let you go and let all this juicy content sink in, I'm sure you're wondering:

> 'But Mark, I don't have the time to speak to so many bookings!'

Let me stop you right there and say **congratulations.**

Congratulations and well played; because there are thousands of hospitality business owners right now, who would love to be in the same position as you. In all the bustle of running your business, don't forget that this is a good problem to have (gratitude rocks).

So, if you find yourself panicking about how to deal with all this extra demand then simply **hire a new member for your team to do this for you**. It's the obvious and most sensible solution; there's no reason why your business can't grow and perform in the way that you want it to.

There are always numerous ways in which you can reinvent your hospitality business model - deal with one guest booking if you need to. Even large-scale projects can be broken down into the simplest of processes, as discussed in the beginning of this Playbook.

And don't forget, while you're on the phone to those wonderful guests of yours (growing your legacy, no doubt), always have the four magic words at the tip of your tongue:

'Do you know anyone?'

GET IT DONE

It's the final round! And this is something you can do **right now.** Don't worry, this book isn't going anywhere.

Your task is to pick up the phone and call a new booking which hasn't checked in yet. As you're speaking to this guest, politely mention those four magic words to them. Don't just drop it into the conversation; make sure you weave it in naturally.

If you haven't got any new bookings lined-up, then you can call a previous guest who you know has had a fantastic stay with you in the past.

Run through the same 'Do you know anyone?' script, as explained in the Relationships and Networking Chapter.

I want to see some instant wins for you and your business. So, before you move on to do anything else today, **do this first.** And don't worry if it feels a bit scary at first, doing this kind of stuff more often will add to your confidence and, in-turn, massively benefit your business.

Don't forget, success is all about stepping out of your comfort zone sometimes - and small steps like these will often have an impressive impact. Go on, go do this now!

SQUAD GOALS

Squad, by simply picking this book up and kicking back with it over a cup of coffee, or in-between those busy school runs, you're already ahead of the curve and on your way to wiping the floor with the competition. If you've read (or listened) through all the chapters in order, then I hope you can agree with me on that.

I certainly hope so. I don't know if I've mentioned this before, but this is the first book I've ever authored. I guess I'm still getting used to new ways of being uncomfortable, too.

Ultimately, the tactics, tips, and training in this book will help your hospitality business in the short, medium, and long term. And you know what? That's all I've ever wanted. To give back to a community that has been so unbelievably amazing for me and my family. It was about time I paid some of those good vibes forward.

I cannot wait to open inboxes full of your DMs and emails, boasting all about your wins. There is perhaps nothing more exciting than seeing a fellow hospitality business owner smashing those goals out of the pitch!

Just a quick reminder: do get in touch via DM on Instagram or shoot an email to info@boostly.co.uk with literally any feedback and thoughts.

And don't forget to look for our hospitality community on Facebook too: **The Hospitality Community Facebook Group,** where you might even cross digital paths with some of the Boostly hosts I've mentioned in this Playbook (it's as good as meeting celebs really).

Also, I expect you to do your 'homework' and watch all the tutorial videos that are part of the online course, which accompanies this

Playbook. Created especially for you, from scratch, and I'm certain you'll get bags of value out of it.

Finally, all that's left to say is here's to your new direct booking future!

It's been a long game and I know we're all getting those post-match aches. But then there's that **champion's adrenaline** too, right? That's the stuff you need to hold onto - because that's the stuff that'll see you through the growth of your hospitality business, in both good times and bad.

So, keep your heads up, champs. You're officially part of #TeamBoostly and I couldn't be more thrilled to have you on our side.

ACKNOWLEDGMENTS

Give us a cheer for...

To my wife Laura, thank you for always being by my side and keeping me grounded. To my three children, Alfie, Charlie, and Frankie. I hope one day you get to read this book and are proud of your old man.

To my parents, if it wasn't for you there simply wouldn't have been this book.

And finally, you know how they say '**Behind every success is a team.**' Well, this has definitely been the case with this Playbook, which would have ceased to exist without the person who I'm about to mention!

Technically speaking, she's actually going to give herself a mention. Being the writer-type, Neely has been determined to put pen to paper herself and tell you a little bit about editing this book (and working with me) in her own words.

(I've already asked her to be nice, and not give away all my embarrassing stories).

Before I hand over to her for the next few paragraphs, I just want to publicly say **thank you, Neely**.

I have wanted to put this Playbook together for years; but never had the confidence to do it on my own.

Squad, please do look **Neely Khan** up on the wonderful world wide web, when you get the chance. Not only does she have an epic story of her own but she helps others carve theirs, with her hospitality storytelling services. What a cool niche.

Over to you, Neely.

The first time I saw Mark, he was speaking on stage at a conference in London.

His eyes beamed with joy, while every member of the audience was totally transfixed on him. I remember thinking to myself: how can one make email marketing sound so exciting?

I was relatively new to the industry when I started working with Mark, but at no point has Mark ever made me feel inferior to him where business is concerned. I think that's what I respect about him most. There is never any ego involved; just honest collaborative work with the intention of bettering the short-term rental space in every way possible.

There are few people who work as hard as Mark does in our industry. From the outside-in, it seems as though Mark is living his best life, always travelling, telling jokes on social media, and sharing Gifs (ha).

And while some of the above is true, there's actually a heck of a lot of elbow grease involved in Mark's business, not forgetting all the time and attention he pours into his beloved Academy, and all its people.

Granted, this Playbook is a bit different from all the other business reads you might have come across. It talks about soccer and *The Matrix*; and pushes you out of your comfort zone to get things done.

In fact, when Mark first shared this Playbook idea with me, I knew straight away that it wouldn't be for everyone. I knew it'd be for action-takers only; those who are willing to go the extra mile for their short-term rental business, and aren't afraid to take risks in the process.

You know, many people will argue that I'm biased, simply because I work with Mark and am friends with him.

But it's true that anyone who's on the receiving end of his guidance (in business and beyond) is blessed.

He's a stand-up guy who truly cares about the people in his community.

He has lived and breathed hospitality; and has all the scars to prove it.

But most importantly, he is honest and kind and he won't quit until he's helped you make a positive difference in your business.

So, keep this Playbook in your backpack everyday. Pop it on your kitchen worktop to dip into every morning. Carry a copy in your car, or gift it to a colleague or friend.

Because this book truly is a lifetime's worth of learning, experience, and memories, specifically put together to help YOU increase direct bookings. While Mark has been kind enough to thank me for my involvement in this book, I do believe that the entire industry should be thanking HIM for being so unconditionally generous with his support.

Mark, it's been a pleasure.

I'm a better business person (and a little more clued up about soccer!) thanks to you.

Can't wait to help you write the next 10.

Neely

(Book Editor and Friend)

COMING SOON

THE
BOOK DIRECT
BLUEPRINT

Printed in the USA
CPSIA information can be obtained
at www.ICGtesting.com
LVHW011044210923
758625LV00015B/1173

9 781913 284305